CONTENTS

Acknowledgments 5
Introduction...7

The Lessons
It's Not About You..19
Fight the Right Way 31
Letting Go 45
What You Feed..54
Get Out of the Boat 71

The Tools
Open Your Mouth...83
Breathe & Lean Back...93
Happiness is within You 102
Peace, Be Still 110
Give Thanks and Praise 122

The Results
Test to Testimony 135
Constant Companions 149

ACKNOWLEDGMENTS

The writing of this book, while it came from my hardest trial, is a reminder to me that all things will truly fall into place if we just put God first.

I would like to thank my husband and eternal companion for his love and support and for the kick in the pants I needed in order to make this twenty-years-in-the-making dream come true. If it weren't for our relationship, this might never have come to fruition.

I would like to thank my mother for giving me my name. It is a daily reminder of my love for my Savior Jesus Christ and my commitment to represent Him each and every day.

I would like to thank my father. If it wasn't for him, I wouldn't have created the need to "write" to express my feelings and the fire and determination to achieve my dreams. I know he is smiling down on me from paradise.

I would like to thank my children for inspiring me to never quit going after my dreams, giving me so much happiness and the strength to keep pushing through some of the hardest times of my life. And I want to thank my grandchildren for lighting up my life with such joy and unconditional love.

All thanks and glory be to God for giving me this gift to write to help others by sharing my story and calling me to present it to the world.

INTRODUCTION

I've always been told that within your deepest, darkest, and most painful moments is where you will find yourself—your true authentic, unaltered, divine self. It's funny because I thought that I had already been to that dark place. But here, I find myself in the darkest and loneliest of places, and I realize that all the other dark abysses were just preparatory for where I am now. Looking back to those trials, I see I've picked up some divine tools and was reintroduced to some of my gifts and talents that I now find are my lifelines for dealing with this place. They will be the building blocks for how I get out. It's amazing to me how our Father in heaven has set the stage for every single moment in our lives. He doesn't allow us to just go to the next thing if we haven't passed the previous test. Or better said, we will not escape an obstacle or trial if we haven't truly learned the *whole* lesson that was meant to be learned within it.

That is where I am right now—relearning a lesson, and when you go through it the second and third time (more like tenth time for me), it knocks you off your feet even harder. It's like being in the ring with an opponent that you thought you beat and would never have to see again. Yet, he has called for a rematch, and *this* time, he is prepared. He has watched the previous fight, studied your moves, gotten familiar with your strengths, but even more familiar with your weaknesses. *This* time when you get in the ring, the surprise is on *you*!

That's me. I unknowingly stepped into the ring and received an emotional blow to the heart by someone I trusted. And when I say the blow almost killed me, *the blow almost killed me*! I truly felt as though there was no way that I could come back from the fight that was taking over my mind, heart, and soul.

In the beginning, I was living every day, watching my back to make sure there wasn't yet another blow that was going to come and crush me even more. I was constantly in emotional pain, and my mind was my worst enemy as it played every negative moment stuck on repeat, like a movie. I allowed myself to be sucked into that reality and let the repeat reel play, going over everything in my mind each moment of the day. It's like I was hypnotized by it and didn't know how to change my thoughts. I was captured in that "victim mentality" way of thinking. I was enraged at how simply being connected to someone, would allow for their wrong choices and bad mistakes to affect me to this degree.

I felt completely broken and empty inside and didn't think that I could change anything. This was just my life, and I had to let it play out as if I was an actor on set instead of the author who was writing the script. I kept telling myself that I was the helpless one and that I was the victim. I should be upset, sad, depressed, hateful, angry, and any other negative emotion that I could think of acceptable for someone that had been lied to and betrayed like I had been.

It felt good at first to keep harboring the pain and lashing out whenever I felt like I needed to, to the one who hurt me, like I was getting back for all they had done. Going back in my mind and bringing up every single memory and situation, where I now realized, was part of the betrayal. That's what I was supposed to do, right? Get it off my chest. Make them pay for hurting me. Not allowing them to forget the hurt and pain that they had caused and making sure there was no time within the day that it wasn't brought up, wasn't remembered, and wasn't talked about. Because being the victim gives me the right to drag out my healing for as long as I want. No one should be able to say a thing to me because "*I was hurt*," "*I was betrayed*," and "*I was lied to*!" And *that* was going to be that, and I dare anyone try to come and say that *I was wrong*! Right?

I held tight to those feelings the first couple of months as things were still playing out and being dealt with. However, when the third month came around, and I found myself still feeling this way and hearing myself saying the same exact things over and over, I realized that something needed to change. Holding on to all that toxicity was not in my best interest nor anyone else's for that matter. I was holding on to so much that it was making me physically ill. I was having anxiety attacks from the incessant worrying over things that I couldn't do anything about.

I even noticed that my prayers were negative. I spent most of my time crying about what had happened, identifying myself as the victim, being helpless, and pleading (more like begging) for God to take all of "*this*" from me. Make my life better, the way I thought that it *should* be. I questioned Him repeatedly as to why I had to endure this type of pain. Haven't I endured enough?

I remember one time specifically where I got so angry with God that I screamed at the top of my lungs, "Why are you doing this to me?" "What have I done to deserve this?" "All I want is to be happy! Why won't *you* let me be happy?"

After screaming at the top of my lungs and letting out such hurt and pain in those words, amidst my sobbing, I realized something. I just finished yelling at God! In that moment, I remember feeling so awful, so embarrassed and ashamed. Then it came to me. He wasn't doing anything, and I didn't *deserve* it, but I am the only one that can control my happiness. The light bulb went off, and I understood that I was doing things *all wrong*! I realized that all of what was happening to me was not for naught but was happening for my good. Even if it was brought on by someone else's faults and mistakes, I could *still* use this opportunity to become a better version of *me*. I knew that I needed to surrender to how God wanted this to play out and what He wanted me to learn from this awful situation.

It was then that I realized that part of this lesson was what I needed in order to give up my need to control everything. I thought that I had done that, but quickly saw that, even when I thought I was giving my issues over to God, I still had a solid hold on them and never completely let go. My hands were still gripping onto the problems just as a child grips onto a favorite toy when their mother tells them it's time to put it away. My hands were in the "death grip," and they were turning red and getting blisters because of how hard I was holding on. I believed (with my type A personality) that I *had* to keep my hands on the problem to make *sure* it was being dealt with in the way that I felt like it should be dealt with. I realized how bold and cocky it was of me to think that I knew what's better for me more than God who created me. Just writing that makes me feel ashamed, even now. I knew better than to question God, and in that instant, I was not only questioning Him but downplaying His authority. To think it would be okay for me to disregard whatever His plan might be, because my plan was better.

Boy, am I glad that we have a forgiving God!

I immediately tucked my tail (as my mother would say) and went back to my prayer closet, and from that moment on, I started praying a different way. I prayed for God to show me a better way and to provide me with what I needed to get through the pain without harboring hate and to be able to forgive. I soon started to feel different—calmer, less uptight, and an ease now came when I prayed. I started to feel an openness to this new relationship that I was creating, not only with God but with myself. I started to discover things that I had learned and been taught in church and in my life coaching classes that I now could use while in this dark space.

I remembered the tools that God had led me to years ago, that I now realized, were preparing me for this very moment. They would be key to bringing me closer to my Father in heaven and to understanding my own divinity.

I remembered my Reiki energy teachings and the fact that I have the divine energy within me to heal myself and others through the ultimate authority and spirit of my Savior Jesus Christ. I remembered the significance of gemstones and crystals and how I can even utilize their energy to bring peace, focus, clarity, and positivity to my life.

I started being drawn to different preachers, sermons, and spiritual quotes. And each day, God would point me to a message that I desperately needed to hear and implement within my life. It's like I was eating at my favorite buffet and being presented with one favorite dish after another. I would find a pastor that would preach a sermon that would speak to me exactly where I was in that moment then that pastor would lead me to another, and another until finally I got reunited with my favorite female pastor.

I had purchased a few of her books *years* ago, and the minute I started listening to her sermons, I just couldn't get enough. She resonated with me and spoke to my soul as if she knew exactly what I needed within each given moment.

And with that, I started on a part of my spiritual journey that wasn't just about reading scriptures and going to Church. But it also included studying and pondering what I read and applying it in my life the way that God would have me to, practicing it and making the necessary changes in order to live it! You see, when we are called to do something great and live in our purpose, we sometimes are brought to our lowest low in order to finally *see* the lesson that has been there all along. It's just that until we are ready to *see it*, we disregard it, and it gets filed away in our minds for later.

This clearly is my *later,* and I'm choosing to *learn the lesson* and apply it *this time*! Unlike some books you read where the person has gone through something, learned the lesson, and comes back to you to report how they now are living their best life. This book right here is going to take you through my journey as I'm going through it. You are going to be able to experience the "aha" moments that I've already seen in the last five months before I started this book *and* any additional "aha" moments that I'm going to have in real time as I encounter them.

This book is going to be me sharing my life in the realist way possible on paper, in black and white, as I go through one of the hardest times in my life. And while I will be sharing, I'm not going to get into the specifics of the what happened, who did it," and "how come" because quite frankly, I think that's irrelevant. Hurt and Pain comes from all forms and all people. The focus of this book is on the "what to do," "who to turn to," and "how to overcome."

I pray this book will give whoever reads it the confirmation that *everyone* goes through stuff, and some stuff is harder than other *stuff,* but with Jesus Christ and our Father in heaven in our lives and having our backs, we can get through *anything!* I'm not saying the journey won't have its fair share of pain, fear, struggle, anger, contentment, and even hate. B*ut* when we learn to put down our wants and surrender to God completely and allow Him to do what He *knows* is best for us, we will be able to start feeling those little glimmers of calm and peace.

I can tell you from experience sometimes slowing down, putting your hands up, giving it all over to God, and then being *still* are the best things you can do, even in those moments that you are the most scared. Because it is in that moment of true and total surrender that you are learning the most important lesson—true faith is what God has always wanted from us. It is then, within that moment of true faith, that He knows we fully *trust* in *him*. He can show us our path and who and what we were created and called to be. He will clearly and divinely show us what we must do in order to come out of the trial with a testimony and how to turn our mess into our message while giving Him all the glory. With that said, I give you a front seat ride in my darkest of times in the journey that I feel will ultimately lead to my brightest light.

THE LESSONS

IT'S NOT ABOUT YOU

I don't know about you, but it's all about *my* feelings when I've been hurt. I need for my thoughts to be heard and things to be in order to get over what's been done to *me*. I was *all up in my feelings* after being hurt, thinking about all the times I've been hurt before. Like when my parents got divorced, and we had to move back to my mom's hometown in the middle of my junior year of high school. When I suffered through unexplained infertility in two different marriages and I was diagnosed with Graves' disease. And, how being a people pleaser seemed to be an open invitation for people to continuously take advantage of my niceness, disrespect and mistreat me, and I could go on and on. I thought about how I felt like I had almost given license for others to hurt me. I sacrificed my feelings most of the time in lieu of pointing out the faults of others. I think being like that gave the wrong signal. Instead of indicating that I was an understanding, forgiving, and loving person, it was taken as weakness. After that moment of reflection, I went back to reality and how I was so livid to be hurt to this magnitude at this point in my life. I allowed myself to play into the "woe is me" victim role and did a pretty good job of it.

I think my Father in heaven was getting quite tired of it though. One morning as I was fixated on the details of how I had just been hurt, I heard a distinct whisper, "This is not about You." I immediately remember thinking "*How is this not about me? I'm the one that has been hurt!*" Then I quickly realized who I was talking back to and where that whisper had come from. In that moment, I took some time to quiet my mind, and I listened to my heart. I realized that *this* situation wasn't about me.

This was about someone else's journey and the simple rule of cause and effect. They made a bad choice (a *really bad* choice) in a time of pain for them that just happened to directly affect me. And as unfortunate as that was, this was actually someone else's consequences from their poor decision. Now, they were being taught their lesson.

But make no mistake. Here I was smack dab in the middle of that ripple effect. A place I didn't want to be and didn't ask to be in. But you know what, that was one of the most humbling moments, I think, I have had this far. My eyes were opened to the fact that even in someone else's mess, I had my own lessons to learn. I could either continue to wallow in my pain and the "why me" feelings, or I could get myself together, really look at the situation, and see what was there for me to learn.

I knew it wouldn't be easy, and that's an understatement, but if I could get through it, it would be so worth it. I've always heard and been taught that you become stronger and wiser through your trials. That there is always something to learn from them. And if you can just get laser-focused on what you can glean from the lesson that is presented within the trial, it will build your character in a way you never could without having experienced it. I realized that the only part in this that I could control was *me*. How I thought about it, how I dealt with it, how I talked about it (if I talked about it), how I went about getting over it and moving on, and how I could allow God to use this as an opportunity to have me grow and stretch within my own spiritual journey.

When I tell you there was a *lot* for me to learn and revisit within myself that I thought I had fixed, *there was a lot*! I think each trial we encounter in our lives stretches us a little bit further in different ways and aspects. I honestly didn't think that some of the issues still existed. However, after some deep contemplation, they were pointed out very vividly. I realized that I had a problem with wanting to be in control. I didn't trust others with getting things done and especially not to my specifications. I realized that I was a people pleaser and that I looked to others to make me happy, safe, and secure. I realized that I pointed the finger at everyone else but never looked at myself. Somehow, I tricked myself into believing everyone else had the issues and never suspected that I did too. Not once did I think that I had lessons to learn and things I needed to change. At this point, I had to open my eyes, stop whining, crying, complaining, feeling sorry for myself, and playing the victim.

Once I identified the areas that I needed to work on, I gained some of my emotional and mental strength back. Just by taking the time to put my guard down and get comfortable with admitting that I wasn't perfect and that I, too, had flaws, allowed me to feel empowered in the process of changing for the better. I knew that it was time to really get down and dirty fixing my issues (which means, it was going to be painful) and deconstruct what I thought was my somewhat perfect life and start the rebuilding process, keeping only those things that served me. And all the things that didn't, I would get rid of, letting them go and releasing the attachment that I'd been holding on to as part of my identity.

It's crazy how we can't or won't let go of a personality trait or habit that doesn't serve us simply because we've been carrying it around for so long. It's a sort of self-sabotage that we do to ourselves. I immediately knew that I needed to change that. I had already identified that I was a people pleaser. This stemmed from my childhood (like most of our issues). But I would say it with conviction, "This is *me*. "It's never going to change."

However, in looking at how much toxicity I've allowed in my life from that one personality trait, I now recognize it as a character flaw. Nothing in my life has benefited from me being a people pleaser, absolutely *nothing*. If anything, it has become an extreme place of worry and disgust for me, something that I've wished I could be freed from many times. It comes on like autopilot. Once it's on, I don't know how or have the strength to turn it off.

I've often found myself wishing I could be more like certain family and friends that could say no and speak their mind without a care in the world. I'm not talking about them being nasty for the sake of being nasty but speaking their mind and not allowing others to dictate how they should be or act. I honestly, have *never* been able to do that, *unless* you mess with my kids. If you mess with my kids or someone else that I love, I can become "Mama Bear" quick, fast, and in a hurry.

But if we are talking about me, *I always* have put other people's feelings in front of my own, and others take advantage of that. It's put me on the back burner and allowed me to be disrespected and with my own consent. Within this trial *not* of my making, I realized that I could make it about me in a more positive way. I could choose to take this time to change some things and become a better me. I asked God to show me what I needed to work on and where I needed to rebuild within my own self in order to become the woman He created and called me to be.

Now, I'm sure you just sighed an "Aw, that's so sweet." But let me just say this, be careful about what you wish for because after that prayer, my journey got even more bumpy, and I was so not ready for it. It's almost as if when you pray for God to show you, the way He shows you is by allowing more circumstances to come in your life that test you and your faith. So more of what I didn't necessarily want seemed to come into my life—more uncertainty, more negativity, more situations that tested my patience and tolerance. Which all put me in an uncomfortable and uncertain place in my life. One thing about me is I don't like feeling uncomfortable in my own skin, and the journey I was on was not at all about feeling comfortable. It was the direct opposite, and *that* felt extremely lonely for me. Working on yourself is one of the hardest, and at times, most painful things that you can do but can be the most rewarding once you get through it. When you take the time and energy to dive into uncovering what makes you, *you*—good, bad, and indifferent—you are able to then remove the things that don't serve you, accept the things that do, and incorporate even more positive things that you want to see in your life. It allows you to nurture and cultivate those things that make you the best version of yourself. And when you are at your best, you can give your best.

The "not knowing" what is to come, that is part of every journey. And it's done with this type *A* personality kicking and screaming. You see, *I have to know* what's next. What's more, *I have to have con-*

trol. If I don't, that's when that uncomfortable feeling creeps up and remember, I don't like that uncomfortable feeling. I must be prepared with a plan *A*, *B* and *C*.

Unfortunately, that's just not possible to obtain with this type of "self-work." It's a learn-as-you-go-trust-in-God's-process type of thing. And, as I mentioned before, this girl has a hard time in the letting go department even when it's the omnipotent, all-knowing being that created me, nudging me to do so. I tried to accept the fact (for like the hundredth time in my own mind) that this mess I found myself in was *the* opportunity to once and for all deal with my own demons I was still carrying around. And when I really thought about it, I realized that it was time to stop running and face them. However, I knew that I had to go about this process the smart way, with rules for myself so that I wouldn't be digging an even bigger hole for my heart to sink in.

First, I decided I wouldn't tell anyone in my family (except for the two that were already somewhat involved), and I wouldn't tell any of my friends. Why you ask? Because when you are going through emotional turmoil, your feelings are everywhere, and feelings are fickle. One day, I might be mad or angry, the next, I might be sad or frustrated.

What comes out of my mouth in those moments might be harsh, nasty, hateful, and irrational. Only *I* know that those are just *words* and the result of whatever I might be feeling at that moment. It doesn't mean that I really *feel* that way all the time or that I'm going to *do* whatever I said when I was venting.

When you express certain things to others, they take you seriously at every single word you say. Sometimes, they even expect you to go through with all you shared to them. And when you don't, they come at you almost like an interrogation as to why you didn't. Giving *their opinions*, which you didn't ask for and you *don't* need.

Let's be real, you are already full of emotions that are all out of whack. You, in turn, are a wreck. So, just leave the "peanut gallery" out of it. Ultimately, you want to go through what you need to go through and make whatever decisions because of what *you* feel and what *you* can deal with, no matter how they look to other people on the outside. What it all boils down to is *you* must deal with the person(s) that hurt you, not anyone else.

So, it's totally your choice. If you keep all the *ugly* to yourself, then you don't have to worry about having to deal with all that *extra* from other people including their relationship with the person(s) that hurt you, which could change their relationship because of what you've told them. Most often, family and friends hold on to their anger out of love for you, so if you don't tell them, you don't get their emotions involved where they really don't need to be. Just take it from me, *tell no family or friends* unless they already have a part in the issue you are dealing with.

Now, let me also warn you, by taking this route, it's going to be extremely *hard* and *painful*. You will have moments that you feel totally alone and like you can't take on one more hurtful thing. And *it will suck*! But just embrace the *suck* and know that it won't last forever.

I remember having panic attacks because of all the stress, emotions, and crazy thoughts that I had to deal with daily. The panic attacks were the worst—the incessant shaking in my legs and my body that I could hardly move, the hair on my neck standing up, my heart pounding out of my chest so hard that I could almost hear it, goosebumps on my arms, my body heating up as if I had just stepped into a sauna, and the worst part, my mind bringing forth every negative thought that it could find to make the anxiety and worry heighten. At times, it could be suffocating. I felt like I just *had* to tell *someone*. Instead,

I reminded myself what I was avoiding, just dealing with it by myself. After letting that sink in for a few minutes, I was able to stop myself every single time. I slowly learned to deal with the pain in complete secret from the rest of *my* world. On the outside, to everyone else, I looked like I had it all together and everything was peaches and cream with a side of rainbows and roses. Little did they know I was going through the darkest time of my life and hating every minute of it.

Now for the second rule. I decided that I was going to finally learn how to put my trust completely in *God*. Although this is something that comes so easy for others, *I knew* this was going to be a battle between my soul (ego) and my spirit (divinity). And I wasn't excited to go through the mental tug-of-war that I knew I was about to have. *But* I knew that it was time that I finally get this, because *this* was most certainly part of *my* lesson. I needed to learn how to fully trust in my Heavenly Father with no worrying, no stressing, no trying to still work the issue out on my part.

Instead, I needed to give it over and then simply go about thanking Him, praising Him, and doing whatever He prompted me to do without thinking anymore on working the issue. I had to let go of the outcome and have complete faith that He knows what's best for me and whatever comes from it will be for my good.

I knew that the *only* way that I was going to be able to do this was going to be putting God first and giving God *time* in my life. I chose from there forward to be consumed with taking in and filling my spirit with His word. And not just leaving it there but implementing it within my life and consciously choosing each day to put *God* first and allow Him to direct my steps.

I allowed *His* love to offer the peace and calm I needed to get through the pain I was going through. I knew if I gave my life to Him and insert Him in everything that I did, every choice that I had to make, every emotion I chose to have that He would heal my hurt, heal my relationship, and heal me from myself and the negative personality traits I allowed to follow me since childhood all at the same time. I knew that in giving Him dominion to do *His* will in my life, that I would be able to realize my biggest dreams all while giving Him the glory. Either way, to me, it was a win-win even if I had to go through *hell* and back to get there.

FIGHT THE RIGHT WAY

In putting all my trust in God, I realized that I was going to have to learn a better way to cope with all the negative feelings I had. I was going to have to find some way to change my thoughts and the negative movie reel that was more than happy to show the whole entire ordeal within my head *and* do it on repeat mode. I knew there was no way that I would be able to let go without having some way to fight off all the emotions that bombarded my mind. I felt on edge every day. My stomach was in knots as my mind drifted back to certain instances that I wanted so desperately to forget. I had this constant fear that some other issue was going to be uncovered that would cause me even more pain and heartache. I was so stressed that I could hardly sleep, tossing, and turning throughout the night and even having bad dreams that I couldn't remember but that would have me waking up drenched in sweat.

And the way I was fighting was tearing me up inside. I mean, I don't even consider it fighting. It was more like cowering down to fear and still identifying with a victim mentality. And *that* wasn't working. It was just making me feel even more insecure, unworthy, and quite frankly, like a failure.

So my answer was to pray and ask God what He wanted me to do and for Him to show me clearly how I needed to change. I got the feeling that I needed to change up my morning routine. I was already getting up an hour early and incorporating prayer, Scripture study, Reiki alignment, and writing down my goals.

So I decided to add listening. I listened to sermons, motivational talks/videos, and positive and uplifting podcasts as part of my morning routine. I figured I needed to have positive reinforcement pretty much all throughout the day in order to keep my thoughts right. Because, if you didn't know, your thoughts become things. The more energy you give to a thought, the more it grows and is manifested in your life.

Therefore, I needed to make sure that my thoughts were positive and uplifting. I didn't need any more negativity in my life, that was for sure. I started off with one pastor then I was led to another and another until I was led to a famous female pastor that I immediately felt a connection to. I loved how she delivered her messages, and I remembered that I even had about four of her books. That first sermon led me to more and more, and I wasn't *just* listening to her sermons in the morning but was listening to them all day long. I couldn't stop finding more sermons that applied to me. I would even play them while I was sleeping, hoping that they could speak to my subconscious as well so I could continue to receive the lessons within my spirit as I slept.

I was getting so much from her teachings that I started taking notes in a small mini notebook and dedicated it to my spiritual journey. I wanted to have a place to write down everything that I was learning from *all* the different pastors that had come into my life and was teaching me so much. As I wrote things down that touched my spirit, it stuck in my brain a little better.

I was even able to recall some of it when I had bad thoughts enter my head. Along with writing things down, I was learning new ways to pray, praise, and even listen to my Heavenly Father. To be completely transparent, I would get so frustrated with myself because a lot of these new ways that I was learning were so different for me. I felt very uncomfortable implementing them at first. Talking to my neighbor and praising God out loud opposed to my beliefs in my head. That's not the way that my Church taught me, and if I'm to be honest, I was taught praising out loud and such was irreverent.

But it didn't *feel* irreverent to me. I felt something special when I would give praise out loud and when I would raise my hands to confirm it. The more I allowed myself to do what felt right to me, opposed to what I had thought was the right way, the more I found myself saying Amen out loud and feeling totally comfortable in doing so. Although I was in new territory, I felt strongly that this is exactly what I needed. I knew that I just needed to dive in and soak up whatever goodness this would lead me to.

Shortly after that, I came upon a sermon given by my now favorite female pastor that spoke on "How to Fight Like a Christian" and felt led to listen to it. It was so eye-opening in the way that it gave detailed instructions on how to let go of things that you can't change and can't handle emotionally and to turn them over to God. I listened to it three times in one day. I took notes feverishly each time I listened.

That sermon, I believe, changed the entire trajectory of my life while in this dark space. I had *never* been taught to let go and let *God* in the way that this pastor explained it. She said to let go and Let *God fight your battles for you*! I had never heard of God fighting battles for you before, and in this, my darkest moment, that sounded so good to me. Like something that I definitely needed to learn how to do. It means to totally and completely relinquish your problems (battles) to Him in prayer through the authority of Jesus Christ and *leave them with him*!

In her sermon, she explains that when we truly cast our cares to our Father in heaven, we shouldn't worry, and we most certainly shouldn't fear because He has your back entirely and will *not* fail you. She warned that God's time is not our time and that he might not be early with an answer/resolution, but that He would always be *on time* with it.

She continued to warn that His resolution might not look exactly like what we were expecting. It might look completely different from what you might have been asking for. It might be a different job than what you were praying for. It might be facing a hard decision longer than you care to. It might be getting a different diagnosis than you hoped you would get. But, because it comes from God, you will automatically know without doubt that it *is* exactly what *you* need and maybe with time, you will see that it is even *better* than what you were expecting. After listening to that sermon, God led me to even more sermons of hers and other pastors that delivered a similar message. That just affirmed to me that it was a lesson that I not only needed to learn, but that I had to learn. I instantly knew that *this* was the second most important piece of this whole entire mess that I had been placed in. And I was determined that I was going to ace it!

I'm going to confess that this LDS convert learning how to shout out glory and praise and talking out loud (sometimes even screaming) in order to rebuke the enemy was very different for me. So was raising my hands to the sky and asking God to help me in those times I felt defeated and confused. But I knew that if I was going to change my relationship with Him and learn how to fight this battle like a Christian that I would need to do whatever needed to be done. And quite frankly, nothing that I had done on my own up to this point had worked. So, the next best thing, *no*, the *only* thing to do was to change my course and fight like God was teaching me to fight.

It was uncomfortable at times (and still is), but I incorporated a different way of talking and relating to God into my life slowly but surely, without judgement, criticism, or thinking that my old way was the *only* way to worship. With my continued efforts, each day I learned a new tool like keeping my mouth shut when something bothered me or not complaining about my circumstances and instead taking it to God in prayer. I was starting to get some of the basic concepts under my belt and implementing them in my life whenever I felt the negativity creep up. Now, I had days that were harder than others. I might go back to feeling that fear, anxiety, and worry. However, I would pray and ask for help, and to be able to relinquish myself to God and trust in Him completely. I then would graciously accept my do over when waking up the next day, instead of taking for granted the fact that each day is another chance God has given us to do better than we did the day before.

Let's be real, *change* is *not* easy, especially when you've been doing it your way (whether right or wrong) for so long. I'm currently forty-six years old as I write this, and I've been doing "me" the way I've been doing "me" for all that time! I've practiced these habits daily all these years. My mind is so comfortable thinking and feeling the way I've taught it to think and feel. I've taught my mind that the only way that something is going to get done right, is if I do it. I've taught it that if I please others, they will in turn love me and treat me as I treat them. I've taught it that I must have control of everything for me not to fail. And, I've taught it that for me to be happy, I need to make others happy, so they provide me with the positive accolades and words of affirmation that *make* me happy. So trying to dismantle that in order to implement new concepts was difficult! And if I'm being completely honest, it was one of the hardest things I had to do. I had to be on watch with my thoughts twenty-four seven. And what's crazy, you don't realize how many self-limiting, negative beliefs and sayings that you think of daily until you start actively managing them. I caught myself thinking negative thoughts like 90 percent of the time, and it was truly exhausting trying to manage that.

And the way that the negative thoughts would just be randomly and strategically placed was very interesting. Well played, Satan, well played.

It was like they were just dropped in my mind in the middle of a positive thought. Know this, the enemy is here to seek, kill, and destroy. Any way he can do that to make us miserable like him, he will do. He knows our strengths and our weaknesses. And he knows how to trip us up to take our attention away from something positive and immediately turn it negative.

He does it so seamlessly which is why we always need to be on guard of our minds. When we enter this battle with Satan through our trials, we must know going in that he will try everything to get us to give up. He knows that you are in pain and focusing on the hurt within the journey. He knows how we think and how *hard* the process is. He is hoping you will eventually slip up and allow him to get into your head. That is why giving our troubles over to God and allowing Him to fight is *the best decision*! It is imperative in order to win the battle!

It took me going through this process to realize that God has better vision than we do. He's got infinite vision and can see all that the enemy is trying to do before he even does it. He also can see what our decision will be if the enemy does, in fact, succeed in tempting us or throwing that curve ball (or two) into the mix.

With God's infinite vision, He will strategically fight for us and thwart off Satan's plans. When you really think about it, isn't it awesome? *God* is fighting for us. We are talking about the omnipotent being that spoke this earth, this universe into existence is working on *my* personal issues in my life, simply because I asked Him. That still puts me in complete awe!

God isn't much different from us when it comes to parenting. It's just that He is 1,000 percent better at it. Just like we don't want to see our children suffer, He doesn't like to see us (His children) suffer. If our children come to us with a problem and need our help, we don't just turn our backs on them. We do all we can to help them because we love them.

That goes the same for our Father in heaven. I mean, heck, those parental feelings had to come from somewhere, right? And this is evidenced in the following scripture.

> Ask, and it shall be given
> you; seek and ye shall find; knock,
> and it shall be opened unto you.
> (Matthew 7: 7, KJV)

When I focused and really contemplated this scripture, I felt like I was able to let go and completely *trust in him* and *in his process*. When I truly *let go*, I felt a peace enter my spirit. I felt the tension release in my neck and upper back, and I could feel my spirit exhale.

That was *the* first time in months that I didn't feel uptight, anxious, and tense. It almost felt like a physical switch had been flipped, and I was now working from a different place within me. No longer was I operating out of fear and angst, but rather I was operating from a space of pure faith and confidence. I knew I had nothing to fear if I was actively and consistently doing my part, continuing to put God first, believing in His ability to handle anything and everything that I gave to Him, and staying in gratitude, praise, and worship.

Replaying in my mind "No weapons formed against me shall prosper" was something I adopted on repeat during this trial. It helped to calm my nerves with the letting go and trusting in God portion. That was one of *the* hardest parts of this whole journey, trusting in God to handle every facet of the issue for me and trusting in His process and timing without wanting to have my hand in it. I had to learn to watch, check, and change my thoughts as well as to *shut my mouth*. I had to refrain from getting antsy and wanting a "progress report" from my Father in heaven just because I wasn't used to not having control over my problems.

I hated sitting in that uncomfortable space. One big thing about God fighting your battles is that you can't *see* the battle being fought. You have no idea what the strategy is, what the next move is, and when and where it's coming from. You truly are looking at nothing, trusting that God is doing everything in the background. No matter how awkward this waiting in the balance felt like, I was determined to let Him handle my battles while I handled what I could and that was my feelings and emotions. I tell you, learning how to refrain from voicing my discontentment, concerns, and pure distrust was extremely hard to do. In fact, it was dang near impossible. But I took me changing very seriously, and I could see that being *that* person who constantly reminds someone of what they did and how badly I've been hurt because of it wasn't helping anything. It was making it worse. Instead of mending the wounds, I was reopening them.

Simply put, no one likes being reminded of the things they have done wrong that hurt someone they love. And it doesn't help in the moving forward process because it constantly brings you back to the exact place of origin from being hurt in the first place.

That was *not* my intent. However, that is how it was taken by others at times. When I look deep down, I think the reason I felt the need to voice everything was because I didn't want to look or feel weak. I already felt so betrayed and like the people that were an intricate part of the situation already saw me as such, and I didn't want that.

I later identified that as my "ego-soul" talking. When our Father in heaven fights for us, many times it might feel like a silent and invisible battle is going on. Our job has now been realigned to not worry ourselves with the actual fight but to give God praise and thanks knowing that the fight is already won and that *we* will be victorious. Learning and embracing that lesson was a huge undertaking for me. But by watching my thoughts and keeping my mouth shut, I was able to see the signs that He started presenting to me. I believe He did this in order to *show* me that even though I might not SEE anything happening, change WAS happening. And He knows those signs gave me life. They are what allowed me to hold on a little longer and wait for a victory.

Trusting in God should be an automatic thing that we do without hesitation. He is *the only* one that knows us better than we know ourselves. I honestly don't know why it was so hard for me. Trusting in God is literally all we have—the knowledge that He can do all things through our faith in Him and His Son Jesus Christ.

In the Bible, it clearly states if we ask, we shall receive (refer to the scripture Matthew 7:7). I think another piece to that is the fact that we can't just have a sit down with our Heavenly Father and ask all the questions. We can't pick up a phone or send a text asking, "Hey, God, how's my problem coming along?" or "Have you fixed it yet?" We can't ask "How much longer?" or "How are things going to look once you fix it?" That would be awesome if we could get that inside scoop, right? It would give us even more confidence and reassurance that our issue will be and is being handled accordingly.

But, of course, that's not how it works. *We* must show our faith, and we need to show Him that we *believe* beyond a doubt that He is working everything out for our good. We need to go about our business, forgetting the thing that we've put in His hands while having no fear, no angst, or anxiety, just peace. So, what do we do after we have attained full trust in our Father in heaven to fight for us? Keep reading, the next lesson is a doozy!

LETTING GO

In wrestling matches, when they have a tag-team match, one wrestler of each of the teams is in the ring as they start the match. The other member of the tag team cannot enter the ring until they are physically tagged in by their wrestling partner. Then they switch up, and the wrestler that was standing on the sideline goes in the ring. The wrestler who started off the match is now on the sideline. That sideline wrestler is not to help the wrestler in the ring by any means while they are outside of the ropes. If they do, it's considered a violation. The sideline wrestler can *only* help the wrestler in the match *if* and *when* they are tagged in. So for all intents and purposes of this analogy, it's *hands off* until I let you know that I need your assistance.

Well, the same sort of rule applies when we turn over our issues to God. We are to let Him work through it and resolve it. And *if* and *when* He needs us to do something other than trust, believe, show gratitude, and praise him in the process, He will let us know, or in other words "tag us in."

And *how* will we know if we've been tagged in? By the Holy Spirit, of course. He will let us know when we need to do something on behalf of our Father in heaven. However, until you hear that still small voice or feel that loving prompting, we are to have our hands off of the situation. This principle right here is where I was stuck for a long while, having trust enough to let go and *completely* go on with my life without feeling the need to check up on and check in with my Heavenly Father daily was hard for me.

And I was a mess. I was extremely uncomfortable with the letting go process. I would let go a little here and there, but most of the time my hands were on the issue, very reluctant to let go and give over full control. Not wanting to be in that uncomfortable space that I talked about earlier is what drove that fear of letting go. And when the rules are one person in the ring at a time, me constantly jumping in to see if my help is needed is *not* a good look. Because then

I'm causing myself a penalty, and possibly upsetting God's plan and maybe even setting the process back.

I'm embarrassed to say jumping in is something that I got good at because I did it *all of the time*! I wanted to jump in and get in a couple of jabs here and a few punches there because of course He can't do it without me, right? At least that's what it felt like to me. I felt like I had to do *something*. I couldn't just pray and ask God to take on my issue that I basically was too weak, too hurt, too broken to take on and not at least try to jump in here and there in the times that I felt strong enough to help out.

However, this is exactly what was keeping me from fighting and healing the right way. And the stress of it all was breaking me down. You see, sometimes the best thing you can do for yourself is to take a step back and let things play out. Yes, it is totally uncomfortable, *but* when you learn how to step back, take a breath, and allow God to make the moves, you will learn that you can trust in what is being brought to pass.

I know for me, sitting in that uncomfortable space was torture. And because I didn't initially have the knowledge of what tools to use to not allow my feelings to dictate my actions, it led me to do things out of fear and haste that I usually regretted later. It had me doing things that were completely out of my character. I was slowly becoming someone I didn't want to become. All because I didn't want to sit in that space and feel helpless.

You know the space I'm speaking of, right? That space where you wonder if you are being played again, lied to again, taken advantage of, and betrayed again. That space where you know that, while you are just sitting there, the same person that hurt you might be out there hurting you all over again. That space where you feel as though you can't do anything to protect yourself. You feel as though you can't take anymore, and you are about to explode. That is the space where you feel your blood boiling and the hairs standing up on the back of your neck while goosebumps grace your arms. *That* space where you feel like you are suffocating in the unknown and being sucked into an even deeper abyss.

I've learned through my situation that acting out of that space called fear is *not* good for you or for the situation. I know all too well the feelings that fear give us, *but*, before you let those feelings build up and take you to a place you rather not go, the *best* thing you can do is sit in that space (I know, but just hear me out). Breathe through the feelings, realizing that they are *just* feelings, taking note that feelings are fickle. They don't last.

Some feelings might not even be real. You might have some of the feelings you have based on thoughts that are not even accurate. And then again you might have feelings that are totally valid for you but aren't facts for the other person involved. Like when at times you say that something someone did or said made you feel a certain way. That person might not have intended for their words to affect you the way they did. However, it all boils down to your perception of their words and the situation. And we know all about perception, right? Perception is your reality, but very well might not be *the reality*.

This brings me back to the statement that feelings aren't facts, and believe it or not, we can choose to change them. We can do this simply by breathing through them, letting them go, and focusing your mind on something else.

Here's an example of what I mean. Have you ever been driving somewhere, like dinner with your spouse? Something comes up in the conversation and an argument ensues? You fight like cats and dogs in the car and all the way up to the restaurant doors. You are steaming mad when you give the hostess your name and the party that you are meeting. You are seething through your teeth as you walk to the table, but it's all smiles, hugs, and laughter the minute you see your dinner party. And for that one to two-hour dinner, everything is A-OK.

In that moment of pure anger, you were able to control and diffuse the argument and even managed to maybe enjoy yourself for that amount of time. And in some cases (depending on how serious the argument was to begin with) you might even leave, temporarily forgetting that you even were mad. Then, you can decide to either drop it or pick it right back up once you get in the car. It's completely your choice.

If you start thinking back on what made you mad in the first place and allow those feelings to start building up again, then it's obvious you will just get right back to the argument where you left off. But, if you choose to let those feelings stay contained, stay diffused, and come back to the situation later, you might find that your initial feelings have subsided and maybe even changed, and you can talk about things differently at a later time. While in a mindset training, I learned that feelings only last for ninety seconds *if* we don't feed into them. The more we give them our undivided attention and focus on them they build intensity. What we feed grows. If you can learn to sit still within your feelings giving no energy to them for ninety seconds, you will find that they will pass through you, and it will be much easier for you to focus your mind on something else.

Another way to explain this process in a more spiritual and visual way is that negative feelings belong to our soul (our ego self). If we learn to lean back out of those negative feelings, we allow our spirit (our divine selves) to replace them with God's love, giving it a new thing to focus on. Quite frankly, I feel like I've allowed my feelings to dictate a lot in my life. I've done a lot of silly things that I wish I could take back because of how I felt or how I thought someone made me feel at the time, key word being "at the time," again, demonstrating that feelings are ever changing.

I used to always use the "how someone made me feel" as justification for my actions. I would lash out, making accusations and assumptions, because I *felt* that they made me feel some kind of way. Again, allowing myself to be completely out of character, doing things that I would never do if I was in my right mind. I would usually reflect on the situation and think how I should have thought things through better and done things completely different.

That's when the "should-a", "could-a", "would-a's" crept in. You know, how you think of all the good stuff to say/do *after* you have made a fool out of yourself. But at that point, it's too late. Feelings are the culprit of a lot of dumb stuff being done. If we just had ninety seconds to breathe through it, focus on something else, heck, even walk away, those feelings wouldn't be the same feelings anymore.

Amazing, huh?

I sure thought so. It's even more amazing when you try it out. So make sure you remember this little tip the next time you get heated about something (I'll go into exactly how to do this a little later).

When we can get a hold of our feelings, it's so much easier to fully let go. To loosen up that "death grip," open our hands, and allow God to work on our struggles, our battles, our mistakes wholeheartedly. He can't work them *his way* if we are holding on to them trying to work them *our way* at the same time.

I know it's scary, but once you remind yourself that our Father in heaven can do *all things*, and *nothing* is impossible for God, it *should* give you that little wake-up call that our problems are no match for our *God*. He *loves* us, and He knows what's best for us. He would never lead us down a road that wasn't for our good. *His* eyes are eternal. They see *everything*—

past, present, and future! And we are only able to see what is physically in front of us and what we *think* is going on. But *God*, He *knows* what's going on within every single situation in its entirety. Simply put, there is no better person to have in your corner, working your issues and fighting your battles *but him*!

Once I truly grasped that, I realized that I need not fear. Loosening my grip was something that I didn't just need to do but *must* do. By doing that, I would be able to get direct guidance from my Heavenly Father through the promptings of the Holy Spirit if I listened and chose to see the signs that He sent to me. I know it feels like you are losing control. But, my friend, when you let go and let God, you are gaining control and a *lot* of it!

WHAT YOU FEED

An old Cherokee is teaching his grandson about life. "A fight is going on inside me," he said to the boy.

"It's a terrible fight and it is between two wolves. One is evil—he is anger, envy, sorrow, regret, greed, arrogance, self-pity, guilt, resentment, inferiority, lies, false pride, superiority, and ego." He continued,

"The other is good—he is joy, peace, love, hope, serenity, humility, kindness, benevolence, empathy, generosity, truth, compassion, and faith. The same

> fight is going on inside you and inside every other person, too." The grandson thought about it for a minute and then asked his grandfather, "Which wolf will win?"
>
> The old Cherokee simply replied, "The one you feed."
> —Native American Tale

I love this tale because it gives a visual of how powerful our thoughts are and that whatever we focus on, we bring more of into our life. This concept right here has taken me such a long time to fully grasp and implement into my life. I'm a born problem solver, planner, and organizer. My brain is trained to look for the problem and then immediately look for all the ways that it can be solved. Although that is a great trait to have for some things, it's not the best trait to have when referring to inner thoughts and being able to focus on positive ones.

I'm not sure when it started for me, but 99 percent of the time, I look for and expect the bad in things. I'm that person that whenever my manager calls me in their office, which currently is a conference call since we live in different states, my first thought is *What did I do wrong*? That is my first thought *every single time*! I know I don't have any reason to think that something is wrong. I know that I haven't done something unacceptable or wrong at work. Still, my first thought is that I'm being called in for something negative.

Unfortunately, it doesn't stop there. I'm the girl who sees the glass half empty and thinks out of a sense of lack rather than abundance. I'm the pessimist that is an optimist for everyone else but me. I've struggled with this for many years and even went back in my brain to try to figure out where it started.

And I think I found where it all began.

I remember as a small child my thoughts were the sky is the limit. I could do anything that I set my mind to. I just knew that I was going to do something *big* once I grew up, and I was excited even though at the time I had no clue what that might be. I was thinking regular kid stuff back then, model, singer, dancer, or actress. And you best believe I would practice all of them.

I remember getting my little sister to take Polaroid (yes, Polaroid) pictures of me modeling on almost a daily basis. Then, I would take some of her. We called that our sister photo shoot. I also remember pretending as though I was singing on stage at a music awards show and even preparing an acceptance speech for the award that I *would* win. I reenacted my favorite daytime soaps, practicing for the day that *I* would be in the spotlight.

In high school, I remember choreographing dance routines when I was on the drill team. And I knew I would be the next Paula Abdul. I had a very healthy and positive imagination when I was growing up. I had this way of placing myself in that imaginative space and truly *feeling* and *seeing* myself attaining that dream. I was such a happy kid.

Looking back, I think I know where it all stopped for me, when my new reality of "things never work out for me" started.

It was when I was told by my parents that they were having marital issues and were on the verge of getting a divorce. I was devastated. I instantly felt helpless and that there was nothing I could do to save my family (as if that was my job). From that moment on, I was made much aware of what trials and tribulations were and what money problems looked like. I no longer was your normal twelve-year-old tween. I now had to grow up and help my mother with my little sister and be accountable and responsible for many things at a very young age.

My childhood innocence was no more. I was dealing with real issues and most of the issues were negative. It didn't help that I saw firsthand how good people got treated badly and didn't get what they wanted or deserved. And by good people, I mean my mother. My father did so many awful things to her and our disjointed, dysfunctional, and broken family during their divorce, and I *saw* him get away with it.

I believe going through the grown up stuff at such a young age was definitely the catalyst for pushing me out of my childhood, "anything can happen" state of mind into a very negative outlook where negativity became the norm for me. I'm honestly not even sure how so many good things happened to me while I was growing up with the negative mind I had. I guess my Father in heaven was looking out for me knowing it was nothing that I chose but more a situation that chose me.

As an adult, I realized that my childhood thoughts of becoming an actor, singer, dancer, or model were just *not* me. Rather than working hard to find my calling, my passion, I succumbed to "this is my life" syndrome. I almost embraced the negative self-talk as if it was a protection from being let down. Because if I don't expect to obtain the things I really want, I won't be disappointed when I don't get them.

Because I had flipped that negative switch on in my head, that is how my life played out in almost every situation. I always focused on what problems existed first and even began to tell myself *that* was my gift. My talent was to seek out and fix problems.

I began to embrace it, and let me tell you, I got to be extremely good at it. I would have a plan *A, B, C, and D* in my mind for pretty much all situations. I labeled it as having a "back up" for the "back up." And that was my signature statement. I prided myself in being so good at solving problems and thought it was something I could make money doing as my full-time business instead of corporate America.

So I decided at one point in my life that I would start up an organization business and offer my services of solving "problems" (clutter) for other people. But from the start, I thought of every bad thing that could happen. I thought about how I might teach them to organize, but they might just go back to their old habits. To be honest, the thought made me a little miffed that someone might not be able to retain what I taught them. I would have to continuously come back to teach them. That is crazy because I should have been thinking about that as repeat business. Instead, I was thinking of it as a *problem*, glass half empty and full of negativity.

When I came across the Native American tale, it really opened my eyes. I started to see that although I could speak optimism into other people's lives and show them how negativity was bringing them more negativity, I wasn't doing the same for myself. I was doing the exact opposite of what I was telling others to do. I'm not sure if I even realized that I was being a hypocrite in not practicing for myself what I worked so hard to instill in others.

I knew that I needed to change. But as I mentioned before, change is hard and changing your *mindset* is even harder. It's a constant job to watch your thoughts. I mean we have anywhere from fifty thousand to seventy thousand per day. That equates to thirty-five to forty-eight thoughts per minute. And when you are trying to corral all your thoughts in order to toss out or change the negative ones, it's a full-time job!

So I started on the journey. Over time, I just stopped being as diligent and found myself years later dealing with the exact same issue. This time, I got a bunch of self-help books thinking they would pull me out of it. And I read every single book that I got, took notes, and said I was going to commit to implementing what I had learned.

But again, I ran into the fact that it was a constant battle in my mind. I couldn't keep up with trying to put out all the negative fires. So right back I went to focusing on the negative and getting more of it.

Fast forward to the fall of 2018, when my world was turned upside down, and I was in the darkest place that I had ever been in my life. I *knew* that something had to change. I knew that part of that change had to include tackling my negative thoughts. That had to be dealt with once and for all. Life is a test, and God doesn't let you move on to the next "grade" until you past the tests and final exam in your current one. Which I think is why I felt like I kept coming around full circle to this same place of knowing that I needed to change my thinking process but not knowing how to do it.

However, this time around I got serious about it.

I started asking my Father in heaven to lead me and show me what I needed to do to get something positive out of this very dark trial I found myself in. I soon received a confirming prompting that *this* was the time that I needed to fix my thoughts once and for all. And this time, I listened!

Number one, I knew that I was *not* going to be able to fix *anything* without God leading the way. I'd been down this road umpteen times knowing that I could do it all by myself. Not sure if, because of all the self-help books I had read, I thought I knew all the things or what. But now, I knew that all of that was a complete lie. Turns out I didn't know anything. If I wanted to get out of this abyss with something gained other than tears and the tissues to wipe them, I needed to get serious and go all in as if I was going into battle.

So, the first thing I did was pray.

I spoke it out loud and gave the battle over to God. I prayed and let Him know that I loved Him. I knew that *He* knew what was best for me and how I would be able to fix my thoughts once and for all. I asked Him to show me the tools I needed in order to take down this demon that was coming after me and my family. I asked for Him to take on my battle and fight the way He knew how, but to also allow me to go through the journey fighting the adversary for my mind back.

Over the years, I had allowed Satan to take this negative thinking of mine and use it against me in all areas of my life. He knew this trait about me better than I did. I think he must have done some extra studying on this go around, because he knew every single way and every context to have me thinking negatively about something.

So I knew that I would need to bring out the *big guns* in order to defeat him and claim victory. The only "being" good enough, clever enough, strong enough to defeat Satan is God and His Son Jesus Christ. I knew what I was about to do was going to be hard. It was going to be stressful. It was going to take some serious mind watching and focus to catch the bad thoughts before I started to believe and speak them. And the big thing was, I promised myself that I wouldn't give up and wouldn't quit no matter how hard it got until I succeeded at eliminating my negative mindset and limiting beliefs.

I immediately started being aware of every thought. When I captured a positive one, I would try to hold onto it for as long as possible. I would focus on it, elaborate on it, celebrate me having the thought, basically doing whatever I could to practice how to focus on the positive until I started to believe it. At first, I felt like this was a stupid exercise, and it would never work. One huge reason was because I had so many thoughts and, out of the many, the majority were negative in some form.

I started out slow and challenged myself to capture one negative thought and replace it with at least three positive thoughts as soon as possible. But if it was a serious negative thought, like some type of limiting belief, self-talk, or downing my marriage or other relationships, then I would have to break out with five to seven different positive thoughts and/or gratitude to replace the big negative thought that I captured.

Why did I want to replace the bad thought? Because everything in this world is made up of energy. Absolutely everything. Even the inanimate objects that we sit on, eat on, write with, write on, the computers we use, the ground we walk on, your car, plants, trees, rocks and even dirt. *Everything* has energy within it—even our thoughts. So if you are giving out negative thoughts, you need to follow up a negative thought with a positive one that gives off a higher energy vibration to combat that negative energy of the bad thought.

The thought is that, even though we might slip up and say some negative things, we can counteract that negative energy with positive energy so that it negates the negative "bump" in the road. It allows us to continue a new way of positive thinking until we hit our next bump. I guarantee you will be using these tools once again. Because the cycle *will* repeat over and over until we have mastered the art of "watching our thoughts" and replacing the negative with positive before it has a chance to change our reality.

Being laser focused on our thoughts forces us to become more aware of them and to have a choice of continuing within the thought before it slips into the feelings/emotion's realm. Once we have mastered choosing our thoughts and what energy we are going to give to a thought, we then hold the power to make better choices with our next thoughts. Our thoughts are up to us. We can either take this new opportunity to continue to focus on thoughts just as negative as the ones we captured and released, *or* we can choose to focus on good energy and allow for the positive thoughts to flow.

And how do you get them to flow you ask?

Once you focus your mind on the first positive thought, you continue to focus on it even more. It's almost equivalent to a positive "brain dump" that you would normally write on paper; therefore, "brain dumping" out of your brain. But in this scenario, you are dumping *into* your brain all things positivity. I know this all sounds a little weird, as will some of the other things that I talk about in this book (just thought that I would give you fair warning), but all of what I am saying is what helped me in my darkest hours. And as awkward as you feel when you start to implement some of this mind-set work into your life, the more you do it, the easier it will come to you and the better you will get.

We've *all* heard the term what you think about, you bring about. Or what you focus on, you bring on (okay, so I think I made that one up. But you get my point). I think a lot of times we downplay those expressions as if they don't work. However, that is all we are doing each day, getting back the things that we are giving out on the same vibration that we are giving off. If we want to change our lives, we need to first focus on our thoughts. Everything starts as a thought. *Everything*!

Here's an example, and you might even have experienced something similar as its pretty common. You know how when you are shopping for a new car, and you've picked out the make/model/color and all the extras you want on it? And you might even have picked out how much you want your monthly payment to be (I totally did). Right after you think about the car you want, suddenly you start to see a ton of *that* car on the road. Now, it might be a different color and not have all the extras as outlined, *but* it is the car.

I know this happened to me when I was dead set on getting my Volkswagen New Beetle after having gotten in a very bad accident some years ago. After getting in my mind the exact car, color, extras, and payment, I then headed off to the dealerships to search for this specific car. It was so easy to walk on the lots, and if they didn't have exactly what I was looking for, I would walk right off. But I also started getting frustrated because none of the dealerships happened to have the New Beetle with all the bells and whistles that I wanted. If they did, the monthly payment wasn't where I wanted it to be.

I even remember one car salesmen telling me that I probably wouldn't find that price because of the extras and that I wanted it to be 5-speed manual shift turbo (even though I didn't know how to drive a manual car at the time). I just smiled at him and did a quick "bless and release" and captured that negative thought, released it, and replaced it with my thoughts that God could do anything.

After going to way too many cars lots to count, I finally lucked out. One lot not only had the color of "*my*" new Beetle, but they also had the extras. It *was* a turbo 5-speed, and get this, icing and cherry on top, it was even within the price range that I had preset for a monthly payment—*booyah*! Something similar could have happened to you. I love using this analogy because so many people can relate to it, *and* it's a great way to show the power of the mind and how being on the same vibrational frequency can manifest into your life whatever is aligned to be manifested at that time.

Another way I heard this same concept explained was in a sermon I was listening to by my favorite female pastor. She likened our abundance of gifts and blessings to Christmas. She said to think back to when you were a child making up your Christmas list. You would put any and everything on that list knowing that Santa was going to bring them to you. On Christmas morning when you woke up, you would run downstairs to see all that Santa brought. You would see all the gifts under the tree wrapped just for you.

She said our blessings/gifts are somewhat like that, God has already given us all our blessings. They, just like the Christmas presents, are out there in the universe just waiting for us to see them, choose them, and open them up. But, just like the version of little you on Christmas Day, you don't open all your gifts at once. You might not even see some of your gifts at first.

I don't know about you, but I used to take all *my* gifts and make a pile and stack them around me. Then I would pick which one I wanted to open first and would continue in the same manner opening the rest of my gifts until I opened them all. If they needed batteries, and we didn't have the right kind (Sidebar: It's so heartbreaking as parent to realize that you dropped the ball with batteries. Either you forgot to get them all together, or you got the wrong kind.), I wouldn't get to play with the toy right away. So even though it's opened, it still hasn't been played with.

The same holds true for our gifts/callings from *God* as we get older. It's like an adult Christmas morning. All our gifts are under the tree just waiting for *us* to see them, choose them, unwrap them, and use them. It's not that we aren't realizing our gifts. It simply might be we haven't gotten to *that* specific gift yet. It might just be that you picked other gifts/talents to "play with" first, and you must finish cultivating that one in order to realize that you have yet another purpose to fulfill or talent to develop. Then when you get within that same alignment, *bam*! It's given to you just like that car you focused on for weeks and brought into your life because of your laser focus and belief that it would be yours.

Imagine what we could do if we had that type of focus and energy with everything in our lives. I think it's much easier to master this concept when you are focusing on positive things. It definitely gets a little trickier when you are trying *not* to focus on the negative things.

First things first, remember the statement "Whatever you focus on, you feed." Therefore, you get more of what you focus on, and that includes the negative things within our lives. When negative things come up, it's almost like it stumps us. We don't know what to do anymore.

It's simple. You do the same exact thing. You continue focusing on the positive things you want to see manifested in your life. And if you happen to slip and let a negative thought back in, you simply bless and release and move on to something positive. And if you *really* want to kick them to the curb, ask help from God. Let Him fix them on His time and in His way. After all, you can do *all* things through Jesus Christ who strengthens you.

GET OUT OF THE BOAT

What's next after fixing your focus? Probably the scariest lesson of all (at least it was for me), you must step out on faith. As said by one of my favorite spiritual teachers, *"You must get out of the boat."* The "boat" reference comes from one of the well-known stories in the New Testament where Jesus was walking on the water in a storm. Peter saw Him and said that he wanted to walk on the water too. Jesus told him to step out of the boat and come to him. Peter stepped out of the boat, totally focused on Jesus Christ and started walking to Him. However, he lost his focus on Jesus for a quick second when his attention was turned to the storm and all that was going on around him. He got scared and started to sink. He cried out to Jesus. "Lord save me." And immediately Jesus reached out to him and caught him and then said,

> *"O thou of little faith,*
> *wherefore didst though doubt?"*
> (Matthew 14:31, KJV)

Even with Peter having Jesus Christ in front of him and knowing all the miracles He had performed, he still had a moment of doubt that interrupted his faith and caused him to sink. We see how powerful faith can be in that biblical story. Yet, at the same time, our fear can be even stronger.

This is another one of those things that I have battled with for most of my adult life. I have struggled with having complete and undying faith in my Father in heaven. And honestly, I think having that type of faith is the most important thing to our Heavenly Father. If you have *Faith*, everything else including all the lessons that I've shared with you wouldn't be an issue. Faith is the hope for things that are not seen. Therefore, you trust that God will give you what you ask for when you have complete trust in Him. Even though you have no idea how or when, you just know it will be done.

Getting to that point where we have the kind of faith that he depicts in the scriptures, like when He states that if we had the faith of a mustard seed, have you seen a mustard seed? If not, it is extremely small. It's probably on the same scale as a chia seed, yet it's even smaller. Christ states in the scriptures that if we have the faith of a mustard seed, we could move mountains.

You need a refresher of the scripture story you say? Here it goes, remember Jesus was talking to His disciples after they had brought a man and his son to him. The son needed to be healed of issues going on with his faculties (lunatic) and when the disciples tried to heal the boy he was not healed. Jesus asked that they bring the child to him, and He rebuked the devil, and the evil spirit departed out of the child. The disciples then came to Jesus and asked why they couldn't cast out the evil and heal the child. Jesus answered as it reads in the New Testament,

> And Jesus said unto them, Because of your unbelief: for verily I say unto you, If ye have faith as a grain of mustard seed, ye shall say unto this mountain, remove hence to yonder place;

> and it shall remove; and noth-
> ing shall be impossible unto you.
> (Matthew 17:20, KJV)

I've always been so perplexed by this story because it seems so simple, but boy, as it plays out, it's extremely hard. I think I've realized what really needs to be set in place for us to have unshakeable faith. We need to get to know our Father in heaven. We need to start spending time with Him and not just reading his word but studying it, pondering it, and implementing the lessons we learn into our lives on a daily basis. I mean, let's be real. How do you trust someone if you don't *know* them?

And I know that we *should* know Him seeing as though He created us. But here on this earth in our physical bodies, we don't. We must be taught about our Father in heaven and His Son, Jesus Christ. Then, as we live out life, fall, and get burned (many times), we then allow life's lessons to bring us closer to Him. We must establish our own personal relationship with God to know with every fiber of our being that He loves us, sees us, hears us, understands us, listens to us, and ultimately wants the best for us.

We are His spirit children (gods and goddesses). He created us. And just like our parents here on earth, we love our children unconditionally and want the absolute best for them. If they ask us for something, they need to know that we will help them and do all we can to make whatever they've asked for happen for them. God is no different, except He has knowledge and capabilities that we just don't have; He has eyes into eternity, and He knows *all*.

So He most certainly has our back and is ready and willing to do whatever it is we ask of Him if it is a righteous ask and in keeping with His will. Knowing and fully understanding that we should most certainly have the unshakeable faith that could be compared to that of a mustard seed. And I think at times we do have that type of faith. Those are the times where we might see instant miracles after saying a heartfelt prayer. Because at that moment, we had absolutely no doubts that He was listening and that our want aligned with what He was willing to give right at that moment.

I, personally, haven't had many of these moments (*yet*), but I can recall a time that I had a determination to get to my daughter's house that was (at the time) two hours away from me and my husband's home. We were bringing her daughter, our granddaughter, to see her. She was sick with her third pregnancy and couldn't make the drive to the rendezvous place with her daughter's father to pick her up. We were all set for the car ride. As soon as we got on the main highway, we immediately came to a dead stop because of bumper to bumper traffic. We hadn't even gotten out of our hometown good and *bam*, traffic. Our GPS showed that we would be in traffic for the next seventy-six minutes.

My husband and I looked at each other and were like, "Oh, heck no!" However, I knew that my daughter hadn't seen her sweet little baby girl in three weeks because of being sick, and I was determined to get to her house that day. We waited in traffic for about fifteen minutes before phoning a friend and her husband to see if they knew of any alternate routes that we might be able to take once we got moving a little bit. They gave us a couple different routes. Once we eventually got to the exit that they mentioned, my plan at that point (since I was driving) was to take the alternate route and pray that everyone else wasn't doing the same thing.

It was another ten minutes or so before the traffic started to pick up a bit, and we started to creep along instead of being at a standstill. I then felt prompted to pray and ask God to please remove the traffic from the road so that I could get my granddaughter to her mother. I even envisioned in my mind the traffic opening and parting like the Red Sea parted in the movie *The Ten Commandments*.

That was the first time in a long time that I prayed with such faith, and I just *knew* that a way would be made for us. And sure enough, almost instantly after I said "Amen," the traffic started to pick up speed, and then a little more, and then a little more. In about five minutes after saying "Amen," we were going full speed. The traffic continued that way with just the normal highway ebb and flow until we reached my daughter's house, and we didn't even have to use the alternate routes.

I'm sure everyone around me was taking a second glance in our car because I was doing some serious praising up in there. I honestly, could not believe that I had just witnessed an instant miracle. All because of my unshakable faith when praying that prayer.

I think God gives us moments like that to build our faith in a way that we can't deny that it was God. Everything about that moment should have had us sitting in traffic for the next two hours. The GPS even showed that there were three accidents. But as the traffic began to flow, we didn't see evidence of one accident or the cleanup of an accident on the road. Now you can't tell me that wasn't God! And if you tried to tell me I would tell you to try again.

I don't believe in coincidences anymore; everything comes from God's grace and Him sending us signs, no matter how big or small, that He is there for us. God can do all things, and He is a God of miracles if we are willing enough to see them. The more we put Him first, give Him time in our lives and share our testimonies with others, giving Him the glory, the more He will show up and show out for us.

The key to having a close relationship with our Father in heaven is having faith and getting on the same vibrational frequency as Him that *only* you and He share. Once you can tap into that frequency, you will find yourself living in that space of complete *trust*. A trust for our Father in heaven that we can't see or touch, but one in which we can feel His presence and energy in our lives. With that trust, we will be able to experience the gift of peace that comes with completely surrendering into His hands and trusting Him to do whatever He sees fit in your life.

Knowing that there is no need to fear or worry because He knows and sees all! Once you achieve being in this space, you can finally see how easy it is for you to do anything, and I do mean absolutely anything. If it is called of God in righteousness and for your good, His will be done! With all of that said, don't allow yourself to hold *you* back! You have everything you need within you to obtain *all* you've ever wanted in this life. You just need to stay the course. Do your part, and whatever you can't do, hand over to God. Then just sit back, give Him praise, and watch Him work on your behalf!

But it all starts with you *getting out of the boat*!

THE TOOLS

OPEN YOUR MOUTH

Now, I know you didn't think I was just going to share the lessons with you without providing you with the tools. The tools are what helped me implement the lessons and have them become an intricate part of my life.

Oftentimes we learn about the tools, but we don't take the time to apply them. Therefore, we, more often than not, find ourselves right back in the same place learning the very same lesson at different times in our life. You know you have learned the lesson when you are actively choosing to use the tools to bring about the changes needed in your life.

The first tool to go in your toolbelt is "*Open your mouth*," and give God praise and thanksgiving *daily*! My favorite holiday is Thanksgiving. It's not because of all the food that is available for us to chow down on, nor is it because it's my birthday month. I love Thanksgiving because it's a time where everyone is focused on all the blessings they have been given, and in my opinion, it starts the wave of niceties that are found around that time of year.

It's a fact you need to show gratitude for what you already have and give Him praise if you want your Father in heaven to bless your life. And I'm not just talking praise within the confines of your own walls at home. I'm talking about public praise. Start being *loud* about what He is doing for you, and how He is fighting for you and working on turning your mess into a message and your tests into testimonies.

Be *loud* and not afraid to share with others how God is doing a great thing in your life and give Him all the Glory! Like I've said before, there are no coincidences. What you are seeing is true "God winks," "God whispers," and miracles playing out in your life. You need to share with others and let them know what He is doing and how He is working in your life.

Everyone is going through *something*. When we share with others the greatness of a recently answered prayer, the timing of a blessing, or even something small that brought the peace and calm you'd been searching for, it's so they can see that God's hand is working in your life. And if His hand is working for you then He can work a great blessing for them too.

We tend to get so caught up in worrying about what someone will think of us if we are true to our faith. However, what we all need to realize is the more you show up and represent your true authenticity, the more people will respect you just for being *you*. No one likes a fake person, and if you think you've been fooling them with your fakery you need to think again.

As stated previously, everything (and I mean everything) is set up with a vibrational frequency. When you are being true to yourself, others will feel that high positive vibration/energy from you, if you are putting forth fake characteristics of yourself, they will feel that negative vibration/energy from you as well. With everything that you do, you should include God in it. He wants to be a part of our lives during the good times too. Most often, He hears from us nonstop when we want something or when we emphatically don't want something. But we usually don't talk to Him just because.

We need to make a point to give Him praise and thanksgiving all throughout the day. There is so much to be thankful for, and the more we realize it, the better our lives become, and being grateful brings on so many other blessings in our life. Don't make it more than it needs to be. Remember, there is no right or wrong time to praise God.

We don't always have to do it quietly. It's good to let others know how God has blessed our life, from the mundane things to the miracles that make your jaw drop to the floor. Now is *the* time to *open your mouth* and tell others how God lives and that He is showing up and out for you daily.

Speaking and saying things *out loud* is so very important. The symbolism in it goes back to Genesis when God SPOKE this world, this Universe, and everything in it into existence. And if you need a reminder, here you go:

> In the beginning God created the heaven and the earth. And the earth was without form, and void; and darkness was upon the face of the deep. And the spirit of God moved upon the face of the waters. And God said, Let there be light: and there was light. (Genesis 1: 1–3, KJV)

This "speaking it into existence" continued until He made everything within the earth and universe including *man,* and of course, from *man,* He made *woman.* There is so much power in words. What you speak about, you bring about. And it might not manifest immediately, but believe me, it *will* come whether good or bad. We must be careful with what we say because our words are just as powerful for *our* life as they were for our Heavenly Father when He made this universe. Therefore, we must be careful in what we think and what we choose to speak out of our mouth from our thoughts.

Something that will help you whenever you are feeling bad or like the next words out of your mouth are going to be negative is to praise God. When we are praising our Father in heaven, that is the time we can rest assure that we need not worry about focusing on negativity and toxicity. If you are like me, and this is something new to you because of the way you were brought up in the religion you connect with most, it's not over for you. You can be taught how to be more vocal when praising God. Yes, it might feel a little awkward at first, but the more you do it (just like with anything new you are learning), the easier and more natural it will come to you. Then soon you will be vocalizing your praise more often.

And when I say vocalizing your praise, I'm not necessarily talking about the jumping around, waving hands, rolling on the floor, speaking in tongues, yelling and screaming praise. Although *that* type of praise is nothing to be afraid of or think of as the wrong way to praise God. But what I am saying is that you can vocalize and speak it out loud without it causing you or others to feel awkward. You can praise Him by speaking to your family and friends in regular conversation. You can do so on your social media feeds. There are many ways to vocally exclaim that you are giving glory to God for all He has done and *is* doing for you in your life.

And let's not stop there. It's also very important to *tell* others how much they mean to you, how they have touched your life, and how having them in your life has been a blessing. We need to *open our mouths* more and speak positivity into this world and to each other. I truly think our brains are set on a negative default here on earth. That is why it is so much easier to believe negative things from people before you can accept a compliment. It's so much easier to judge ourselves and others and pick out all the flaws and negative characteristics rather than see the good and make comments on that.

We must start seeing the immediate need for positive change, and if we start with praising God *out loud* and being thankful for *all the things*, I truly believe it will trickle down to us seeing our fellow-man in a more positive light as well.

And, boy, do we need that more than ever in this new age of social media where everything in your life is "fair game" for all to see. It appears some people feel that because they can hide behind the screens of social platforms, that is their cue to do, say, post, and comment whatever they want. They don't care if it's nice, nasty, or totally inappropriate because now they don't have to worry about seeing you face to face or the consequences from a snide/rude comment.

Unfortunately, these days, I think some people aren't looking to spread positivity. They are looking to stalk and creep on your social media feeds, wait for the best time to throw you off your game, and post an inappropriate comment. Or better yet, find a post where they can attempt to tear you down and leave negative and toxic comments for all your friends/followers to read and think less of you. There is so much negativity in the world by default and misery loves company and "hurt people, *hurt* people."

That is why it is so important that we share God's love, grace, glory, patience, and understanding with others. It is imperative that we open our mouth and let our positivity flow out into the universe. Just sharing our testimonies and how God worked blessings in our lives might help give someone else the hope they need to go on. It might also give that hater that is always looking for ways to tear people down a reason to think twice before posting negativity on our platforms.

The enemy's agenda is to seek, kill, and destroy. He will use any means necessary to carry out his will. However, no matter what battle you are up against regarding warding off Satan and any of his followers, *you*, my friend, have been given a promise from God that you needn't worry or even get a thought in your mind that you will be defeated in the righteous endeavors of your life. Do you remember the promise in Isaiah 54:17? You don't? Well here you go.

> No weapon that is formed against thee shall prosper; and every tongue that shall rise against thee in judgement thou shalt condemn. This is the heritage of the servants of the LORD, and their righteousness is of me, saith the Lord. (Isaiah 54:17, KJV)

With this promise, it doesn't say that we won't have weapons formed against us, but what it does say is that they won't prosper. So whatever issue you might think is too big, too intense, too messy, don't stress it. Open your mouth and give it to God and allow Him to fight *for you*! And don't you even worry your little heart over that issue again. You can check in here and there through prayer, being sure to acknowledge that you have full faith and trust in Him to resolve the issue.

That's what He wants to see, that we have faith enough to trust in Him and *let go*. That shows our obedience to His word and to His authority. Then praise Him, and let others know that you are trusting and praising Him in your situation, and you will *not* worry or be upset because you *know* that God has your back! Make sure you are being all the way vocal with what God is doing in your life. Share the miracles, God winks, and testimonies that you get throughout your spiritual journey. Because I can almost guarantee you that after you speak it, you'll find that someone needed to hear exactly what you shared. Be sure you are on the lookout for them because I can tell you they are most certainly there.

God wants us to see His work in our lives, so He gives us signs, and that's why most of your prayers get answered by another person or through a show you might be watching or something you read in an article or book. No, God isn't going to come down on our sofa and have a question/answer session. But at lot of times, especially when you are going through trials and tribulations, He will strategically put people in your life at the perfect time for you to receive answers to your prayers.

So learn how to show up more for those around you. Open your mouth to show thanks for all the blessings that God has given you in the past, in the present moment, and for your future. If you do this simple thing of opening your mouth, you will ultimately be unlocking the door for even more favor in your life. So you better stop playing around and get ready because you are about to see what God *really* can do! And last I checked, He can do *anything*!

BREATHE & LEAN BACK

First off, let me say for all of you that might be thinking it, no, the title is not the year 2000 reference to a very popular hip-hop song that told everyone to "lean back" in sync and on beat. So let me just state that right up front. However, it is meant to be shared as an amazing tool that I learned in order to cope with hard things and how not to allow myself to get caught up in feelings. Feelings and emotions can sometimes keep us trapped because we get in a never-ending highlight reel of the words and actions that caused the feelings in the first place. Sitting in a negative space for any length of time is just not good point-blank period. But it most certainly isn't good for someone that is working on staying positive and emitting positive vibrational energy.

To say it again, the thing to remember about feelings and emotions is if you don't feed into them, they only last for a short amount of time. It sounds simple, and, technically, it *is* very simple. The key is not getting caught up in the feelings and the ride down the rabbit hole they can take you on. That is the hard part. Instead, you must allow the negative feelings to pass through you, without holding onto them, giving them any thought, or placing any of your energy into them. Because the minute you engage in them is when you get sucked in.

I for one am all about "team positive," so learning this technique was imperative for me. Therefore, I made it a point to learn how to implement this little trick into my life, no matter how silly I thought it was when I first heard about it (which I totally thought it was silly, and there was *no way* it was going to work). I thought that if I could master this technique, it would bring peace of mind during hard times and ward off my anxiety/panic attacks that come on with the onset of excess stress. I was secretly praying against my own doubts that there was some validity to this practice, and it would be my saving grace!

Would you like to know how it's done? Yes? Okay, so let me share with you this simple technique that I learned from two life coaches and admins of a Facebook group that I belong to. And let me tell you, as I have practiced this technique and perfected it for *me*, it truly has become my saving grace and stops my anxiety in its tracks. Okay, let's go back to the thought that feelings/emotions last for a short period of time, ninety seconds to be exact, if you let them pass through you and don't entertain them. There is an exercise you can do whenever you feel certain emotions starting to overtake you and manifest themselves physically, like anxiety/panic attack or even anger/road rage. You see, something I think we need to remember is that feelings and emotions affect the body as a whole. Just think about when you are getting nervous. Your palms might start to get clammy, and you might feel yourself getting hot on the inside and start to sweat. When you are scared you might feel knots in your stomach, shortness of breath, or even goosebumps, and the hair standing up on the back of your neck.

Feelings and emotions most certainly affect the whole body. When they do so in a negative way, it most always causes stress. And stress causes all types of problems within the body because of the toxic hormones that are released when stress is present. Which is why it's so important to get a handle on our feelings/emotions. "The exercise," it's quite simple. Whenever you feel a negative emotion starting to build up within you, I want you to immediately set the timer for ninety seconds. Then I want you to breathe in deeply, in through the nose and out through the nose. Imagine yourself "leaning back" out of the emotion while you continue to breathe focusing only on the breath. After the ninety seconds, the feelings that you had associated with that emotion will be gone.

Now, if you're like me, you need a visual of this concept in order to grasp it a little more. So think of yourself standing in a line where you are about to do the wave, you are holding hands with the people on either side of you. When the wave starts, you will see and feel when it's getting close to you and when it's about to hit your hand so you can allow it to go through you to the next person on the other side of you and to continue until the end. However, if you drop those hands and step out of the line, you will be removed from the flow, and the people on either side of you will automatically close in the gap so the wave can continue without interruption/hesitation.

And that, my friends, is the idea here when trying to allow for a negative emotion to move through and past you. You step out of the line, allowing for the emotion to continue without you being an active part of it. And because emotions can only exist for ninety seconds on their own without any energy being fed into them (otherwise known as being an active part), once the ninety seconds is up, and you are now focused on something else, that negative emotion will be gone from your spirit. This prevents some of the negative reactions that come from entertaining and reacting to our feelings/emotions.

I know this exercise seems so simple that you're thinking, *There is no possible way that it could work.* But let me be the first to tell you, it does. With the key being you must step out of the feeling and focus your energy on something else. This goes right back to one of our previous lessons "What you focus on, you feed."

This tool is my favorite because it teaches us that not only do we need to be in control of our thoughts, but that we also need to be control of our feelings. And most of the time, we go through life allowing our feelings to control us. When we feel mad, we react. When we feel sad, we react. When we feel disrespected, we react. When we feel betrayed, we react. When we feel belittled, we react, and when we feel hurt, we react.

I can guarantee you that most of you reading this book when you have feelings that you think you must react to, you do so without even taking a moment to *decide* and *choose how* you will react. You just do whatever you are led to by the feeling that you are feeling at that very moment. Not taking into consideration that you might not *feel* that way in thirty seconds, five minutes, or fifteen minutes.

When we don't allow ourselves to take a beat before reacting, we allow the feeling to have power over us and our thinking. The best thing for us to do is to take a moment to see just what *is* the best thing for us to do at that time. And sometimes the answer isn't coming back with an even better clap back. Sometimes the best thing for you to do is do nothing and keep your mouth shut.

I know you are probably saying to yourself, "What? Do nothing?" Yes, that's exactly what I'm saying. Sometimes the best thing in negative situations is for you to *do* absolutely nothing and to *say* absolutely nothing. Instead, do everything in prayer and even to do that in secret. Some battles are just not meant for us to fight as we would normally do. Like I stated previously, sometimes the battle needs to be given to God, so that it can be fought the right way and with everyone involved learning the lesson that is meant for them to learn.

Silence is a tool that I know seems very simple to some. To others it might be the hardest thing for them to learn how to do. You must let people *know* that they *can't* treat you any kind of way, and if they do, you are going to let them have it. Sometimes "going ghost" on a person is worse than snapping on them. Getting upset and riled up only brings the negativity of the situation back on you. It leaves the door wide open to receive even more stress in your life. It also gives a pass for the "reap/sow/harvest" rule to come back on you, also known as the law of karma.

Whatever you choose to call it, one thing is for sure, two wrongs don't make a right. I would be lying if I told you I have never wanted to *go at* someone that was coming for me. As a matter of fact, I've let myself get sucked in a few times and have totally done the clap back. Did it solve the problem? Was the issue put to rest? Heck no, it just made it worse. Now, they feel they must one-up what you clapped back with, and it's a never-ending cycle of negativity and toxicity.

Now there are special situations wherein things might need to be talked through like with family and close friends. And even in those situations, I advise that you don't have those discussions while tensions are high. But, use the breathe and lean back technique to refocus your energy and your feelings. Then take a moment to decide what the next move will be, being sure it's coming from a positive space. And when all involved have had time to cool off, *then* you can have a discussion.

But for anyone else that is *not* an intricate part of your life, your response should be silence whether face to face, text to text, or social media (especially social media). Always be aware of how your reaction will make you and your body feel and *if* the reaction will truly resolve and/or dissolve the situation.

I was scrolling through Instagram one day and saw the following quote: "Do not get upset with people or situations, both are powerless without your reaction."

That is so real and goes back to the old saying, "It takes two to tango." Some people just want to get you riled up for the sake of getting a reaction out of you. Their only agenda is seeing that they have gotten you so upset that you allowed yourself to be taken out of your character. Remember "Hurt People, Hurt people." So those people that want to keep picking fights and going on and on with negativity when you have already gone silent to shut it down will start to see that they will have to stop because there is no fun in it anymore. And that is when they figure out where the real problems lie—with *them*.

Now that you have been taught this tool, place it in your "tool-belt." And please remember, make it a tool that you use often. Use it so much that it restructures how you deal with feelings/emotions so that you no longer allow them to have power over you in any situation. But rather, you realize that you have power over how you *feel* and the power to change how you feel when you need to. It's all up to you, totally your choice. When you start deciding to choose your mental, emotional, physical, and spiritual health over an ever-changing, ninety-second feeling, you will finally be taking back the power that you've been giving away so willingly to negativity and toxicity.

HAPPINESS IS WITHIN YOU

After reading this chapter, you are going to have a totally different way of understanding what it means to "Be Happy." I've always thought that happiness was something that I found outside of me or something that other people provided to me when they did something that made me happy. Boy, was I wrong. I've been searching for happiness everywhere but where it is truly generated. And who would have thought that I would have to be in the darkest place of my life to find happiness. And not just to find it, but to learn that it's not something we need to look or search for.

Happiness is found within *us*.

Happiness is there *all* the time, not just in the positive situations, but in the negative ones too. Happiness is something that is created from within and a direct reflection of what, or should I say *who*, we put our trust in. Happiness is within us, and we just need to learn how to tap into it and allow it to flow into our lives consistently.

It's amazing to me (now that I get it) how much of our power we give away. I've always been taught that things, good situations, and other people are what bring happiness into our lives. If something was off and/or someone was making us feel a certain way (knowing now that no one can make you feel any type of way), that was our trigger to take note that they weren't making us happy.

First lesson in being happy is the fact that it is *your choice* to be happy or not. That's right, I said it. *No one* can make you happy; you choose to be happy. This is indicative of how when we are angry/mad at times and folks want to try to get you out of your funk by making you laugh or talking about something lighthearted. If you want to stay in your funk, it won't matter how many people try to get you out of it, you will continue to remain right there until you choose not to.

So, why is it that we think that being happy is something that we get from the outside? Why do we give imperfect people the responsibility of making us happy? And if we aren't looking for someone else to make us happy, we are looking to our situations/circumstances within this imperfect and broken world to provide us with the happiness that we desire. When you really think about it, it doesn't make sense, does it?

Don't feel bad. I was right there with you, relying and depending on others to make me happy. That, in all honesty, is a very big burden to put on someone. Because when they miss the mark (and they *will* miss the mark at times) and don't make you happy, they feel as though they've failed you in some way. Truth is, no one can make you happy all day, every day, 365 days of the year. Nor, in my opinion, do you want them to. I know you *think* you want that, but believe me, you don't. Simply put, you then give that person or situation way too much power over you and your emotions. And do you *really* want that?

I would much rather feel happiness daily that is not connected to anyone else but *me*. You can *decide* to be happy and change that negative thinking that goes on in your mind. Not only are our minds set to default to negative, they also are programmed to do whatever is easiest with the least effort. In other words, our brain likes to do things out of habit or autopilot so to speak. Therefore, it sheds some light on the fact of why it (the mind) would rather depend on other people to bring us happiness rather than working tirelessly each day to combat bad thoughts and dismiss them for us to hear the positive thoughts that are going on in the background of our minds.

Let's be real. With the fifty thousand to seventy thousand thoughts we have daily, being in complete awareness of these thoughts and removing the negative ones can be a daunting and exhausting task. The brain totally knows that because when given the choice, it opts out of that task pretty much every single time. If the brain is trying to have an easy ride and coast through each day, why would it want to do excess work necessary to clear out negative thoughts?

Which brings me back to the fact that we don't have to search anymore for true happiness because it is found within *us*. I know someone reading this is saying, "Well, how is this true when we have bad things happen to us that affect our happiness?" And the answer is you can still be happy during the trials and tribulations. And believe me I've tested out that theory myself while going through the most difficult trial in my life thus far.

Remember the chapter on feelings and how they are ever-changing? I'm sure you can recount a time in your life where you were feeling down and depressed and didn't want to be bothered by anyone. Then suddenly, something happens around you that makes you smile or even laugh. At *that* very moment you have broken the energy frequency that those feelings of depression were on. You see, happiness is one of our innate gifts from our Father in heaven. It is there for us to tap into at any time. It's just that we get in our own way. We tend to think that controlling anything within us is something that is out of our hands, and it is controlled by what is happening *to* us.

Nothing could be further from the truth.

It was never meant for us to just be sitting ducks for *life* to throw at us whatever it wants, and we just sit back and take it. We are divine beings. We are children of a loving Heavenly Father. That ultimately means that we are gods and goddesses. Because of our divinity, we most certainly do have the authority through our Savior Jesus Christ to speak into our own lives through personal revelation.

We don't just have to sit back and watch life happen to us. We are meant to be active participants. Scratch that. We are meant to be active creators! We are not meant to have the mindset that is going to keep us slave to feeling powerless because that right there is *not true*. However, it *is* what the enemy wants us to believe, which is why he also wants us to believe that we can't possibly be happy unless it involves someone else or something else providing it to us.

Our Father in heaven has given us all we need in order to find happiness within our own hearts despite what we are going through. This can be done even when you are going through hard times. It's just a matter of removing yourself from the negative feelings and allowing yourself to focus on those things that fill you up with happiness. What are your joys, your aspirations, the things that make you laugh, that give you hope? Those are some of the things that you can focus on when you are in a space of negativity and working on finding your "Happy."

For me, some things that bring me instant joy and happiness are nature, animals, laughter, my sweet grandchildren, prayer/scriptures, and music. Whatever your things are, they are now considered your tools to bringing happiness from within. Whenever you need that pick me up or kick in the pants to step out of the wave, you can think on these items and find instant inner happiness.

And once you find it, hold on to it for a bit. Don't just find it and release it because you are setting yourself up to be pulled back into the negativity. Instead sit in your happy place long enough to take that feeling and make it a thing. Remember whatever you focus on, you feed. So for you to find the happiness within and keep it, you must focus on it. This, of course, takes more effort than focusing on something negative.

However, we need to stop shying away from things that take work and aren't easy. This *whole* process called life takes work. But work is what is needed for you to become a better person, the person that God has created you to be. And you surely aren't going to just metamorphosize into that new person by doing and thinking the same old thing you've always thought. You are going to have to choose to change once and for all. And within that change comes hard work, and it will most often than not come with pain. But sometimes, pain is the best place for greatness to appear.

> "Expect opposition, it is needed if you are to become what you are meant to become." (Pastor John Gray)

Happiness dwells within us always. We have the love of our Father in heaven, His Son Jesus Christ within us, and the Spirit of the Holy Ghost, which is our ultimate comforter and provider of peace. That knowledge right there alone gives us access to all the happiness in the world. We just need to learn how to live from a place of divinity and allow our divine selves to manifest within our lives. We need to stop turning to our earthly/temporal selves that are full of fear, doubt, negative thoughts, and beliefs. If we will just trust in God with all our might, mind, and strength and allow Him to show us the way in all things, we will finally find our portal to ultimate happiness that no one can take from us. Stop looking outside yourself for happiness, because the happiness is and always has been within *you*.

PEACE, BE STILL

And there arose a great storm of wind, and the waves beat into the ship, so that it was now full. And he was in the hinder part of the ship, asleep on a pillow; and they awake him, and say unto him, Master, carest thou not that we perish? And he arose, and rebuked the wind, and said unto the sea, Peace, be still. And the wind ceased, and there was a great calm. And he said unto them, Why are ye so fearful? how is it that ye have no faith? And they feared exceedingly, and said one to another, What manner of

man is this, that even the wind
and the sea obey him? (Mark 4:
37–41, KJV)

This is one of my favorite stories of Jesus Christ
in the scriptures and it is the last tool that I'm going
to give you. It's also one of the hardest tools to grasp
the true meaning and implement into your life.
However, once you do, it's the most rewarding as it is
the tool that is the final link that brings together all
the spiritual tools that I've shared within this book.
Just as the story depicts, to have peace while going
through a storm is extremely difficult. It challenges
every earthly/temporal instinct that we've been given.
When we speak of peace, we must also speak on fear
because they go hand in hand. When we think of
peace, we think about feeling calm, being at ease, and
free from disturbance.

Those are indeed true characteristics of peace,
and we normally think of peace when we think of
positive situations and the perfect ending to a story.
However, just like the story in Mark, peace can come
within the darkness of a trial, even while you are still
going through the hardest time of the trial.

However, it doesn't come easy. The only way
peace can come to you while you are going through

a trial and override the fear is through the Savior and having faith in Him.

When listening to a sermon, the pastor said, "We receive from God through Faith, and we receive from the devil through Fear." Therefore, in order to obtain peace within the storm, we must have faith and turn away from *all* fear. While going through trials, Christ doesn't change the definition of peace in order to accept those moments where we experience fear and exhibit feelings of being upset, scared, and even depressed. He gives no passes when He asks in the Bible story, "How is it that ye have no faith?"

In that moment, He truly is completely taken aback by his disciples. He probably was thinking to himself, all the miracles that they have seen performed in the name of God, all of the people that have been healed just by speaking over them and/or touching him, all the revelations and being witnesses to angels coming to speak and our Father in heaven speaking down to the earth, how could they not have faith? How could they be fearful in a storm when Christ himself was in the boat with them? Not only did they lack faith, but they were fearful and woke Jesus with a little bit of (what we would call today) a "tude" (nasty attitude). As if to say, "How can you be sleeping in this storm?" "How can you not care enough about our safety to wake up and do something about this?" "We are going to die out here while you sleep!" "Don't you care about us, enough to save us?"

Now what's wrong with this picture is the fact that they had seen all the miracles that their Savior Jesus Christ had done. Yet all of that went out of the window, and they allowed fear to come in and create doubt. That exact same thing happens when we are way deep in our troubles, and we forget all that our Savior has done for us. We start to fear and doubt that He is with us and that He will save us.

When our situations seem as big and strong as that very storm from the scripture is when we need to in fact, stay calm. When someone attacks us or lies on us, we need to stay calm. When someone stalks us on social media and leaves inappropriate comments, we need to stay calm. Even when someone attacks our family with verbal confrontations, *that*, my friends, is the very time we are expected to be calm like the sea. That is when Jesus is telling us "Peace, be still" like He did to the waters, and they instantly obeyed Him.

You see, peace is the ability to be still and patient in *any* situation. That's right, *any* situation, and you get extra points (remember those) when you do it when you are going through a trial. There is nothing that quite matches having so much faith as when it looks like you are getting beat up in the "ring of life." You want to take matters into your own hands and fight back your way, but instead, you pray. You lift your hands in praise and let go of the issue. You give it to God and have absolutely no doubt that it will be taken care of.

And, when I say, "no doubt," I mean that Amazon Prime kind of "no doubt." You know what I'm talking about. You have "no doubt" that when you click that "place order" button that it will get to you within those two days! You aren't going crazy emailing Amazon's customer service repeatedly asking them for an ETD (Estimated Time of Delivery) each hour until you get your package. And if you aren't doing that for Amazon, then you shouldn't be doing that with the creator of the universe.

Which is why, in the beginning of this chapter, I said that Christ couldn't believe that His disciples lacked faith. He had shown them how he could do all things in all the works and miracles He had done that they, themselves, witnessed. I'm sure if this was in our day, Jesus would have been like "Really? Are you kidding me right now?"

But I'm not going to lie; I totally get how they were feeling in that boat because that is exactly how I was feeling within my trial. I felt like I was drowning, like my lungs were filling up with water with every additional piece of the puzzle that would unfold day by day. I couldn't breathe. The walls were caving in on me. I was slowly but surely being crushed by all the hurt and betrayal.

And I, too, wanted to run to my Savior and ask, "Don't you see all of this pain that's being placed on me?" "Don't you see how I'm being treated?" "Don't you see the betrayal that's being forced upon me?"

In my angered state, I wanted to yell and say, "Why have you allowed this to happen to me?" "Why have you allowed this crushing pain to come down on me when I haven't done anything wrong?" I just couldn't understand why it seemed that my Father in heaven and my elder brother Jesus Christ were okay with me being treated this way and going through this agonizing pain.

In the very beginning of my trial, I wanted so badly to lash out and make people pay for putting me through such gut-wrenching pain. It felt like I was getting beat up emotionally every single day! I wanted to respond back to all the rude and disrespectful comments, voice messages, e-mails, and even the inappropriate DMs that were sent to my Instagram business feed. I felt like if I didn't respond, then I looked stupid, and they would feel like they were winning the battle.

However, as the months passed, I continued to get deeper into studying the word of God. I realized that responding to the childish drama was completely opposite of how God wanted me to work this. You see, as I continued in this emotional and spiritual journey, I got closer and closer with my Heavenly Father to the point where I could feel and hear the Holy Spirit whisper to me so clearly. And one day, when I was about to lower my standards and respond to all the chaos, I heard the prompting, "Peace, be still."

From that moment on, I had a whole new outlook on what that phrase really meant. For me, it meant to stop thinking with the ego/carnal mind and allow myself to think with my spiritual and divine mind. To trust in *God* with all my heart that He had control of the situation, and that I could sit within the chaos and *do* nothing. Not one thing! Letting Him work the problem, His way and on His time, having every confidence that the outcome would be better than anything I could have ever imagined.

You see, as much as we want to believe that we know what's best for us and what's in our best interest, we don't. Our sight is extremely limited to whatever we see in the moment—the right now. But God's view is infinite. He has a view of the past, present, and the future. His view is truly eternal, and He *knows* how every single outcome of every situation will affect our life. Therefore, it's best to leave it all up to the master creator. What we think is best for us and what we think we want is no match for His eternal wisdom and glory.

There are a couple of hymns that outline this very important tool of peace, be still. When writing this book, I felt impressed to share a couple verses of them with you. Singing and reciting these two songs sometimes was the glue that held me together when I felt like completely giving up while going through the hardest parts of my trial. Music has a way of just skipping all the extra and going right to your spirit. And sometimes that's what you need, to *feel* the lesson and understand it from the inside, out. The first hymn is called "Master, the Tempest is Raging," and I'll be sharing the second verse with you.

> Master, with anguish of spirit
> I bow in my grief today. The depths
> of my sad heart are troubled. Oh,
> waken and save, I pray! Torrents of
> sin and of anguish Sweep o'er my

sinking soul, And I perish! I perish! Dear Master. Oh, hasten and take control!

Chorus: The winds and the waves shall obey thy will; Peace, be still. Whether the wrath of the storm-tossed sea or demons or men or whatever it be, No waters can swallow the ship where lies The Master of ocean and earth and skies. They all shall sweetly obey thy will: Peace, be still; peace, be still. They all shall sweetly obey thy will: Peace, peace, be still." (Text: Mary Ann Baker, ca. 1874 & Music: H. R. Palmer, 1834–1907)

That hymn gives me such peace and reminds me that if nature will obey His will, then I must too. This next hymn is one of my absolute favorites. I have sung it many times when I've gone through trials and each time it brings me a different sense of comfort. However, all the other times I have gone to this hymn for comfort I've also expected to get an answer to a specific problem or prayer. And in going through this journey, I wasn't looking for any answers per se, I was strictly looking for peace. And I found it in a way that I never have before. I was given the feeling of true peace, meaning, even if things didn't go the way I prayed for them to, God is still going to be there for me, and I am going to be okay.

I think this is the first time that I allowed myself to get that personal revelation and it *not* make me upset. I truly trusted in God and knew He was looking into my situation with those all-knowing eyes and would bring to pass the absolute best outcome for me. This next hymn I'm sharing with you is "Be Still, My Soul," and because this is one of my ultimate favorites, I'm going to share all three verses with you.

> Be still, my soul: The Lord is on thy side: With patience bear thy cross of grief or pain. Leave to thy God to order and provide; In ev'ry change he faithful will remain. Be still, my soul: Thy best, thy heav'nly Friend Thru thorny ways leads to a joyful end.
>
> Be still, my soul: Thy God doth undertake To guide the

future as he has the past. Thy hope, thy confidence let nothing shake; All now mysterious shall be bright at last. Be still, my soul: The waves and winds still know His voice who ruled them while he dwelt below.

Be still, my soul: The hour is hast'ning on When we shall be forever with the Lord, When disappointment, grief, and fear are gone, Sorrow forgot, love's purest joys restored. Be still, my soul: When change and tears are past All safe and blessed we shall meet at last. (Text: Katharina von Schlegel, b. 1697; trans. By Jane Borthwick, 1813–1897 & Music: Jean Sibelius, 1865–1957)

I pray that the words of that song will give you peace in your heart, mind, and spirit and allow you to give all your trust to God. Knowing He is the one person that will never steer you wrong. He is the only one that has your back 1,000%; you can trust that with your life. I know it's hard at times to give all your control over and not have any clue what the outcome will be. But if you will just pray to your Father in heaven, making your requests and your concerns known, He will take it from there in all His divine knowledge and glory. You are completely safe in His hands. So, go ahead. Give it all to Him and be blessed with the gift of peace.

Then be still and watch what he does on your behalf.

GIVE THANKS AND PRAISE

After all the lessons have been taught, and you've learned how to implement the tools, there is a bonus tool that is key in linking everything together and wrapping it all up in a huge bow. And that bonus tool is, "Give Thanks and Praise." Going through any sort of spiritual journey is a process, and it's certainly not easy.

Every single lesson is just as important as the other. You don't usually learn lessons without getting a little knocked around and banged up emotionally and unfortunately, sometimes even physically. But it's through those hurts and pains where we usually want to change. And the change comes from the types of tools you choose to use. They are key to repairing your mind and spirit from all the hurt and pain that has been inflicted upon you.

In order to get the best healing and rebuilding you want to use the best tools. And if you want the *best*, you've got to go to the source, and that is our Creator. The absolute best tools that allow you the ability to heal are the words and love of God and His Son Jesus Christ. When you have the Godhead (God, Jesus Christ, and the Holy Spirit) in your life working and fighting your battles, you don't need anyone else. All *you* need to do is give thanks and praise. Know without a doubt that the issue is in the best hands possible and *will* be worked out in your best interest.

I used to think that when I said a prayer and asked for help on something that was what I needed to continue to do—*ask*. In my mind, I needed to continue to pray for that same problem or situation frequently and consistently, almost as if reminding God that I wanted Him to work on *that thing*. As if he would forget my prayer, what was I thinking, right? He is *God*; He doesn't forget! However, I would get fixated on something that I felt needed to be changed and would pray on that issue constantly until I saw the resolution. And if I didn't *see* a resolution, I thought God was punishing me or was being silent when I really needed Him.

Something that I just didn't get (or understand) when I first started this personal and spiritual journey was how to pray. I honestly thought that I knew how to pray as I had been taught how to pray from a young age, and totally thought I had it down pat.

> Step 1: Address God in reverence
> Step 2: Give thanks
> Step 3: Ask for what you need/want
> Step 4: Close prayer in the name of Jesus Christ

That's it, all the steps. How could I be praying wrong, right? It wasn't that I was praying *wrong*, but that I wasn't praying *strong*. My prayers lacked faith, belief, and sincere gratitude. It's almost like I was praying too regimented; I wasn't allowing myself to go outside of the previously mentioned steps in order to really get *real* with my prayers.

I was forgetting that *God* was my Heavenly *Father*, and fathers want to talk with their children not be talked at. They want to not only hear about the woes and sorrows and what is being asked for, but also what we are happy and thankful for. He wants to hear that we notice all the things that He does on a daily basis that we tend to look over and just come to expect. He wants to hear that we notice His hand in even the most simplistic things in our life. He wants us to take *notice* of Him in the smallest fraction of how He takes notice of us.

When I was in what seemed like the depths of despair and loneliness, I remember a friend of mine telling me about a movie called *The War Room*. In the movie, they spoke about how every home should have a prayer closet where you can pray in secret like the scripture says. When I heard that part in the movie, I was intrigued because I have read the New Testament many times and couldn't recall a scripture about a prayer closet. However, if they said it was in the scriptures, then I just needed to find it and read it for myself. When I picked up the Bible and looked up the verse, there it was.

> But thou, when thou prayest, enter into thy closet, and when thou hast shut thy door, pray to thy Father which is in secret; and thy Father which seeth in secret shall reward thee openly. But when ye pray, use not vain repetitions, as the heathen do: for they think that they shall be heard for their much speak-

> ing. Be not ye therefore like unto
> them: for your Father knoweth
> what things ye have need of,
> before ye ask him. (Matthew 6:6,
> KJV)

I was floored. How have I just glossed over that scripture and not taken heed to it? How did I not find a need to improve the structure and delivery of my prayer to my Father in heaven much sooner?

After learning the lessons and using the tools, I decided to dig deeper and figure out why I wasn't further along in my prayer life than I was. I figured that maybe a lack of prayer skills couldn't be great for my communication with God. It very well could be the culprit in why, at times, I've felt like I wasn't getting any direction or answers. After really looking at all the steps of prayer, I realized there was something major that had been left off and never taught to me growing up.

Giving thanks and praising God as if your battles are already won.

I lacked the knowledge that we only need to ask our Father in heaven once. After the initial ask, we must then go into a phase of thanks and praise in honor of our God for taking on the situations that were just too hard for us to undertake. Giving them to Him allows us to go forward in peace, knowing that He has our back and will work our issue better than anyone else can. And those battles that you've given him? You know the ones that you've said, "If this keeps going on like this, I'm done" or "I can't do this anymore" or "I'm not strong enough for this, Lord." For those, He not only *fights* for *you*, but He sends the Holy Spirit to guide you and give you peace in the situation.

And from what I can recall in the scriptures, God has *never* lost a battle. I learned one of my biggest lessons when revisiting how to pray. When we continue to pray for the same thing in the same way repeatedly, that is indicative of having doubt. It's almost like you are running back to God and reminding Him each day. "Don't forget what I asked you." "Have you worked on the problem I gave?" "When are you going to get around to listening to my prayer so I can receive my blessings?"

What I didn't remember and quite comprehend is that there IS a right way to pray. And if all you are doing is coming to Him with problems to fix, you just might be missing the true point of what prayer is. Don't forget that God already knows what is within your heart. He already knows what you are about to say in your prayer before you even say it. He wants us to come to Him in prayer to have direct communication with us.

Prayer is an opportunity for us to come to Him of our own free will and invite Him into our lives. Remember, God has given us free will and agency. He is bound by the forces of nature and His own rules He has set for this earth, and He doesn't just come into our lives and change us. We must come to Him and *ask*. Unless we come to Him and communicate through prayer, we are just going through life with the mute button on.

If we want to be spoken to, guided, and given direction by our God, then we need to learn how to come to Him. Then and *only* then will He open all the avenues for us to receive that divine, omnipotent guidance. But most people have been taught that prayer is a time where you ask for things you need/want and a time to complain about all the things you don't want in your life. It's even a time to throw a spiritual temper tantrum because you aren't getting specifically what you asked for in the time frame you asked for it to come.

Don't get me wrong. I'm not saying that we should never ask for things that we want and need. However, what I *am* saying is that you should be switching up your conversation with God just like you switch up your conversations with your wife, husband, mother, father, child, etc. (you get my drift). We rarely go to Him simply for a daily update to just tell Him about our day without asking for anything in return. We don't just go to Him to say, thank you for *all of the things*.

Believe it or not, God sometimes just wants to hear from you to see how you are doing spiritually, mentally, and physically (not that He can't already see that). But He genuinely wants you to talk with Him. He wants to know if you see His hand in your life. He wants to hear that you see *Him* and that you love *Him*! And prayer is *the* vehicle that He has provided us with to communicate with Him directly through the authority of Jesus Christ. That is why, at the end of our prayers we say, "In the name of Jesus Christ."

We must remember to give thanks and praise to our Heavenly Father for doing *everything* for us. We wouldn't be in existence if it weren't for Him. If you are not taking the time out to give thanks in your prayers, you are missing a *huge* piece of the communication process. And to be honest, it's a little one-sided. Although I know that sounds crazy since it already seems like it's one-sided when you aren't talking to someone physically face-to-face. But stop being a smarty-pants; you know what I mean!

Our Father in heaven wants to hear from us *all* the time, not just when we are in crisis or have an emotional battle. And that is why when you are in a spiritual battle, you *must* learn to incorporate thanks and praise in order to do *your* part while He does His. Don't make the same mistake I did with regards to the scripture Matthew 6:6, outlining how to pray. Something that I was bad at was repeating myself in every single prayer. The same opening, the same things to be thankful for (pretty much). Even if my "asks" were different here and there, I would repeat those same asks in every prayer.

That is equivalent of us asking our parents the same question over and over again after they have told us they would handle it.

What I didn't grasp is that once I have asked for whatever it is, I need/want, I can truly leave it with Him. Because unlike us here living this earthly life, He *will* take ownership of it; He won't forget, and He will bless us with IT or something that better suits us and our needs that we might not understand while we are in the moment. Once we leave it with Him, we don't need to worry about it or stress over it because now it is God's to handle on our behalf.

However, if you are anything like me, that is a very hard concept to take in when *you* are usually the one that everyone gives their stuff to in order to handle. You get so used to holding onto everything, fixing everything, finding resolution for everything, and owning the issue, not letting go of it until it's completed. So when you have that opportunity being given to you, it's sort of hard to take in and trust that you don't have to do anything but be thankful and praise God's name. Then, give Him all the glory when your resolution has been realized and achieved.

And for me, I've even felt guilty that I wasn't at least still holding on to the worry of the issue at times. But when I've entered my prayer closet and had intimate conversations with my Father in heaven expressing these feelings, such peace comes over me. I take comfort in the fact that He is helping me simply because I've asked Him to. Just as I would my child that came to me in tears, heartbroken, and out of sorts. If I could do whatever it was that they asked in order to bring them happiness, joy, and peace, I most certainly would without hesitation (within reason of course).

Our God is no different. We *must* take that in and fully *understand that*! We are all His spirit children. He loves us unconditionally. There is nothing that we can do today or in the future to make Him love us anymore than He does right now (that's another awesome quote that truly took me aback when I first heard it). I know that might sound crazy, but it's the truth.

You see, when we each were created, and He blew the breath of life into us, He loved us for *eternity* in that very moment. So there is nothing that you could possibly do to make him love you any less than He is *eternally* loving you right now. So let Him take on your battles, your asks, your issues, your arguments, your heated discussions, your fears, your doubts, and *you let it go*!

All the work that you thought you were going to have to do is gone. The only thing left for you to do at this point is to feel gratitude. Be thankful and *say so*! Start shouting from the rooftops how *good* God is. Allow the Holy Spirit to give you comfort and peace while you wait for your ask to become your blessing. And with that, be thankful, shout in praise and give *God* the *glory*!

THE RESULTS

TEST TO TESTIMONY

I'm sure you are probably wondering why I don't have additional chapters for "The Tests." We all know that there are so very many tests that we go through in life; it would be impossible to list them all. But that's just it. Whatever the test/trial/ tribulation you go through, these lessons and tools apply. When I was first prompted to write this book, I wondered if I should lay out the test that I was going through, the test that prompted all this learning and tool usage that I've done to get to this point.

And notice how I didn't say that I have gotten through it. Because the fact of the matter is, I'm not completely there yet. However, writing this book and going over all the things that I've gone through and learned this far has truly changed me in such a positive way. I realized that the details of my test really didn't matter. What mattered was how I was getting through it and sharing that part of the journey with others. Who would have thought that going through the darkest place of my life is where I would truly see the light? I sure didn't.

When my trial first came to me, I felt like I was hit by a Mack Truck and had an out of body experience watching myself take on that emotional blow. I remember feeling like my heart was being ripped out of my chest, cut up into little pieces, and placed back in for me to figure out how to unscramble them and make my heart whole again. Looking back, I was an example of a functioning depressed person. In my true people pleaser nature, I put on a face of happiness that my-life-is-perfect façade, when I was dying inside.

For me, that was normal. I was brought up being taught by examples from my mother that you can't just succumb to the emotional pain in plain view for everyone to see. You mustn't show *that* to anyone. Instead, you must move through it. You must walk, talk, and be as if nothing was wrong. Smile on the outside while you are suffocating from all the hurt on the inside. There were moments that the pain and darkness was so overwhelming; it was all I could do to get out of bed some mornings. And there were even some moments where I felt like it would be better if I just disappeared. I'm not talking suicidal here but more so imaginatively speaking. It would've been so much easier if I just was able to blink, nod, and snap myself into the *after* of the storm.

I honestly didn't want to have to go through the pain, but I knew the only way out of the *hell* was to go through it. Not to mention because of my perfectionistic personality and my need for control, I *hated* being in uncomfortable spaces/situations. I think I'm a great problem solver for that very reason. I can't stand sitting in an uncomfortable situation. And unfortunately, with *this* particular issue, *I* couldn't fix it; therefore, magically getting to the other side seemed like a much better option.

But of course, that's not how real life works. And quite frankly, I also felt like I'd been through enough tests/trials already. I didn't wish them on anyone else, for real, but I felt like, "Can't someone else take *this* one for me and give me a break?" Like, for real already.

Since the time I was twelve years old when my parents first divorced, I felt like I had to step up and take on the mom role, not only for me and my little sister who was four years old at the time, but also for my mom that had her world come crumbling down on her. I made up in my mind at that young age that I was going to make sure that they both felt loved and had good memories despite all the chaos that was going on.

Quite frankly, I think that is where my tests started, and in my opinion (and yes, I'm biased), it seems like they never let up. I mean, don't get me wrong, there was a little ebbing and flowing, but it surely felt like the minute I was cleared from one issue, another one was lurking around the corner ready and waiting to take its place.

I remember nicknaming myself the black sheep of my family very early on. If I'm to be completely honest, I didn't lay that lie down until I started writing this book. I know that we are given trials so that we can learn, become stronger and wiser from them. But for me, I've felt like each trial came out of left field and knocked the wind out of me when they have presented themselves in my life. I still don't quite get the *why* behind some of them and why it seemed like they were all piled up on me at times. Sometimes, I felt like I was getting the brunt of them because I was being punished. I mean, I had to have done *something* in order to have so many negative situations sent my way, right?

But in the writing of this book, I thought to myself that maybe, just maybe, they were all perfectly placed within my life. They weren't sent just to teach *me* a lesson, but through my pain, I might be able to help someone else through their own trials. When I've looked back on my past trials, I've asked myself many times, "What was it specifically that I was supposed to get from that?" "What was I supposed to learn?"

And in all these many years, I hadn't received the answer until I just finished writing that previous sentence. What was I supposed to learn? Oh, I see it so clearly now. I was supposed to learn that I was never meant to take on all these trials by myself.

My problem was I wouldn't surrender to God. I always had to be in control; I thought I knew what was best for me, even if it was God trying to show me a different path. I was holding on so tightly to what was comfortable so as not to ever get myself in that uncomfortable space. Yet I would pray and pray for Heavenly Father to guide and direct me and then just plain *not listen*.

There were more times than I can count that I heard the still, small voice whisper to me to make a different decision or to take heed to a prompting I was given, but oh nooo. I got good at discounting the whispers of the Holy Spirit as just my own thoughts. And of course, if they were my thoughts anyway, replacing them with an even *better* thought was still a win.

Clearly, I thought my way was the *better* way. If I knew what I wanted and needed and mapped out the perfect plan then surely, I would be just fine. God would be okay with that, right? How surreal is this that I am in this very moment realizing that if I had listened to all those promptings, most of the trials would *not* have existed. Or, if they did, they wouldn't have been to the magnitude that they were. God was *always* with me and guiding me with the voice of the Holy Spirit. I was the one clearly *not listening*. I turned a deaf ear to what He was trying to help me avoid.

I see now how He was trying to lead me to other paths and journeys that would have avoided some of the hurt and pain I've experienced in my life. I disregarded the still, small voice and thought it was just me trying to cop out of doing something because I was scared or because I was listening to other people. I didn't trust that my Father in heaven was actually sending me guidance and that voice wasn't my own, but the voice of deity.

So I chose to pick the harder road by doing it all on my own. That choice led me away from the path that I was supposed to be on for a while, but God always has a way of getting you back on the right path that He created specifically for you. This became somewhat of a song and dance that continued to play out in my life. And when the next trial came, I would repeat the very same cycle. Veering off into my own lane and shutting out the very voice that was beckoning to me to listen for my own good.

It reminds me of Moses leading the people out of Egypt and into the Promised Land. It was only supposed to take eleven days, *eleven days*. But because of them doing what *they* wanted to and getting caught up in their own heads and not obeying the instruction from God that Moses presented to them, it took them forty years, *forty years*!

That is me. Boy, did I go around Robin Hood's barn way too many times. I was entangled by some of the same chains that I had been through before but hadn't learned the lesson to prevent myself from revisiting that space again. My journey in the wilderness has been twenty plus years long with many different lessons that I've learned. I am *just* now coming out of it, learning things about myself and my God that if I had just embraced many years ago, I might already be where I'm still striving to go at this very second.

However, like I said, that's the beautiful thing about our Father in heaven. Even when we don't make the choices that we should and stray off the path, He *always* makes a way for us to find the path once again as if we had never strayed. He will move those puzzle pieces around. He will create puzzle pieces to make sure you *fit* into what you were called to be, even if it's later than when you originally were to have arrived there. Make no mistake, He won't take away any of our blessings; they are *all there*, just waiting a little longer, being placed a little differently, but still there ready to be bestowed upon us.

In all the trials I've experienced so far, with all their varying degrees of pain, going through all of them truly has prepared me for this trial that I'm going through right now. If it weren't for my Father in heaven breaking me, I probably still wouldn't believe that I can do and get through *anything* with the help of my Lord and Savior, Jesus Christ. And I don't think I would be at this place right now, writing this book for someone out there that needs it just as much as I did when I got the prompting to start writing it. For someone out there that is in so much pain that at times you wonder how you will go on and you question if you even want to. For someone out there that thinks no one else could possibly understand, or possibly care. My sweet friend, *I do*! I care about *you*, and I want you to take in my words and know that they were written from a place of complete surrender.

Because right now, as I write these words, I've surrendered to my situation. *I know* that I can't do anymore to change anyone but myself. I've given it *all* to God, and He now fights my battles for me. I've presented my outcome to Him, and I know that He will take that into consideration while giving me the outcome that is *best* for me. That outcome could be exactly what I've asked for or what I've asked for and more. It could very well be something completely different. But I trust in Him and know, whatever the outcome, it will be the very best for me and according to His will. I have decided to have faith, believe, and put my full trust in God knowing that my ask is righteous. He will take it, own it, and fight the fight on my behalf.

In turn, I know my job is to give thanks and praise Him each day, knowing that when the time is right (which is always the perfect time with God), He will show me our victory! My friend, please listen to me when I tell you that it's best that you learn the lessons from your tests because you *will* be repeating them until you do. You will find yourself going around that very same mountain day after day, month after month, and year after year. It might not look or feel like the exact same test each time, but the same lesson is hidden within. As things start to unfold, you will find that you start feeling very familiar within the space you are in. And you begin to feel that negative energy lurking in the background as if to warn you and prepare you for that lesson that you didn't learn before that is coming back around to teach you yet again.

So if you want to stave off having to go through the test more than once, take heed to the test that is before you the first time it is presented. Ask God "What do you want me to learn from this?" "What do you want me to give to others while I'm in this place of discovery?" "What do you want me to say to others going through this?"

You see, another way to heal is to use your gifts/talents to serve others. This was a big part of my lesson. I never thought how I and all my baggage could help others. That somehow, all the darkness I've gone through could be used for good. But yes, even while you are in your darkest moments, battling for your own emotional and spiritual health, you can still be of service to someone else. You know firsthand how lonely being submerged in trials can be. Who better to help someone else than someone who had been right where they are (or even worse) and letting them know and giving them proof that they will get through it?

How powerful is *that* message to someone coming from a person who has lived through the battle? It's very powerful! It's one thing to hear stories of triumph and victory, but it's a totally different deal to be able to see and converse with someone that is currently going through the *fire*. Going through trials is *not* easy, I don't care who you are. However, the positive of it all is there is a lot of personal growth that *can* happen if we seek it out.

Question is, are you ready for that growth or would you rather stay stagnant, knowing that you are destined to repeat it in some way in the future if you don't learn now. For me, that was my strategy for so many years. I would get so caught up in the thought of the pain and heartbreak that a trial would present just by having to go through it. And then to willingly add the additional pain that would come by looking into my soul to find the root cause of it all? Oh, heck to the no!

I remember thinking there was no way that I was going to willingly put myself through any more pain if I didn't have to. And if only I knew then what I know now, having that type of negative mindset is what got me on the pathway of receiving multiple trial by fire lessons to learn in the first place. You see, rather than facing my fears and walking through the fire (remember we must go through it if we want to get through it), I chose to run. And because of that choice to *run* (and by run, I mean run like I was in a horror movie run), I could dodge all the pain that usually comes with personal growth. And if we are going to talk about running, let's talk about how sometimes your journey might feel like a marathon!

Okay, most of them do. And this one of mine? It has been a doozy. It started off being the most painful thing that I've ever gone through in my life but at the same time, the most rewarding. I'm not saying that there aren't still moments of pain, but I've got my tools, and by using them, it's become much easier for me to disengage from the feelings and emotions and just deal with the *real* underlying issues.

I can't even believe I'm about to type this, but I wouldn't have changed this experience in the least bit. And for me, that's somewhat scary to say since I'm still going through it and my *the end* has yet to be determined. However, I know what I want it to be. I feel in my heart of hearts that is what my Father in heaven wants for me too. Pain in any form physical, emotional, mental, spiritual is something that we are just going to have to accept. With physical pain, we tend to be more accepting. We even *trust* that the wound will heal with time, and we don't stress it. We just allow the body to do what it is created to do and heal itself.

Even with physical pain to the magnitude of having heart attacks, strokes, diabetes, limbs lost, skin burned, the body still heals itself. Now the healed portion might not look exactly as it did before. There might be some things that are different, *but* this miracle called the *body* can and will heal. And we trust it to do just that.

But it's a whole different "ball game" when we are talking about emotional, mental, and/or spiritual pain. This pain is one that won't heal itself. *We* must do something in order to heal, and this is the pain that we dislike the most. Because of that we tend to go through life in fear. We're fearful that we are going to run into a situation that will require us to *stop* the marathon that we are running. You know that race to get away from *all of the things* that you are afraid of or just plain don't want to deal with. If we are being honest, these are *the* things that keep us from our own calling and greatest potential. The things that, if you finally stopped and allowed yourself to address them, heal them, and let them go, you would never have to run again—at least not from the pain.

My friends, no one ever does anything great without going through the trials, tribulations, obstacles, and pains of life. Nothing worth having comes easy to us. We must work for it. Remember that most of those hiccups that appear in our life are sent by the enemy to trip us up, to trap us into thinking that we can't, we won't do better, and even throwing in there the ol' "I'll never be able to change." But God allows them, because He knows that *you can* overcome them and be a greater person because of them. You just must make the choice, stop running, dig deep, commit, and *do it*!

CONSTANT COMPANIONS

Throughout my life, I have always shared my trials with people that I've trusted. Most often, that would be my family. I'm not sure why, but I've always felt the need to have someone else's opinion when it came to a decision that I needed to make in difficult and emotional situations. It's almost like I didn't trust myself and what *I* wanted to be able to make the right decision for myself. What I didn't realize (until much later) was that when you invite someone into your life and solicit their advice, you are at the same time giving them permission to be in your business.

As I touched on previously, your problem/situation is then made the topic of discussion whenever you see or talk to them. And they feel like they have a right to be in the know. Now, I'm not saying that they aren't asking for updates out of concern. But what I *am* saying is that *your* problem has now become their problem. And instead of you being able to take what they suggested as just a piece of advice, you have one or two (or more, please don't tell me you have more than a couple) people feeling like they have a vested interest in your resolution. They tend to feel as though they can comment on whatever decision you happened to make and feel some type of way about it. They might even feel like they can make arguments on your final decision and what your resolution was if it wasn't the advice they offered.

My friends, I wish that I had learned this lesson a long time ago, you don't need to tell anyone your problems except *God*. This is sometimes very hard to do when you are going through them because most of us don't like going through hard things alone. So we have that want, almost a need, to share it with someone else so that we aren't carrying all the hard things by ourselves.

That's exactly why I used to do it. I thought by telling someone else, at least I wouldn't feel alone. I could bounce my feelings, ideas, and emotions off someone else to see if I was on the right track. Would they do what I would do, did they agree with how I was handling the problem, and if not, what did they think I needed to change?

It all sounds good when you first think about it. But when you *really* stop and think about all that comes from bringing someone else into your mess, the reality starts to hit. People that love you don't want to see you hurt. And when they see you hurt, their first response is that they want to protect you.

Problem is, sometimes the way they are trying to protect is not what you need or want. And once they see you are not doing what they suggest that you do, they feel as though you don't trust their opinion, have wasted their time and have emotions like you are doing something bad against them. Now, we know that not all situations are cut and dry. They can come in all forms. Some are light and easy to fix, and some are downright messy (like soap opera messy).

But the fact remains that however they come, they are *yours*. Only *you* can decide how you will handle it without the judgement that comes from someone else knowing your story and feeling like you've handled it wrong. The best listener, the best counselor, and the best advisor is God. You will never, I mean *never*, go wrong if you go to God with your trials. He has a team that is ready and waiting for you to ask for their help and tag them in.

When I realized this point, my whole life changed. I was so close to picking up the phone to tell one of my family members or a close friend about me being in so much emotional turmoil. But every time I was about to, I would hear the words, "Stop, don't do it." The feeling was so strong that I knew it was a prompting from the Holy Spirit.

I listened, but it wasn't easy. I was in so much emotional pain that I wanted to do what I had always done, and that was share it, release it, and give some of my pain away to someone else that I could trust. Have someone else to help bear my burden. Not even understanding that the very moment I shared, they would then be vested in a whole different way because they now were somewhat sharing in my hurt and pain as well.

In that moment, I had an epiphany. I realized that doing what I had always done in all the previous situations where I had relayed my anguish to someone else had not turned out well. In some instances, it caused friction between me and them for quite some time simply because I chose not to take their advice. I immediately thought to myself the definition of insanity—repeating the same thing over and over expecting to get a different result.

And from previous experience, my results have always been discord, disappointment, confusion, and regret.

This time, I listened to that prompting and refused to give in to the want, and sometimes my need, to tell my family. Instead, I made a commitment to go to my prayer closet and pour out my soul to my Heavenly Father. Then I would ask for the consolation of Jesus Christ and for the Holy Spirit to provide me with peace, calm, and comfort so I could continue another day dealing with the pain on my own.

In the beginning, much of my prayers consisted of me blubbering through them, ugly crying, my nose so stuffed up with snot I could barely talk. I felt like my heart was literally breaking. And in some of those times, I felt like I just couldn't go on in this by myself. I just had to tell someone.

But again, I received the distinct prompting (and even stronger this time) to refrain from doing that and to trust in God. Weeks passed by with this same scenario going down—me in my prayer closet breaking *all the way down* and feeling like there was no relief coming to me. It got to the point that I questioned if my Father in heaven was even listening.

Then little by little, I would start to see signs, signs that showed me He was listening to every single word that I spoke. I would be talking to someone, and they would say something to me or do something for me that I had asked for in prayer. I would see a graphic on an Instagram feed that was the exact thing that I needed to see at that moment. I would see a sermon or motivational video that would be the first selection offered on my YouTube feed the very next morning that would give me the answer that I had been praying for the night before.

Now, of course, most people would just chalk that up to coincidence. But friends, I don't believe in coincidence. I believe in *God*. A God that loves us unconditionally and wouldn't turn His back when we ask for His help, and in my case, begging and pleading for it. Instead He showed me, and I mean *he showed me* that He *was* listening, and He was answering my prayers. He even answered prayers by sending people my way that gave me spiritual upliftment and motivation just because they felt a strong prompting to do so, having no idea how much I had prayed for that exact message.

As the days went on, I started to feel that I had constant companions in my life. They were listening to every single thought, emotion, feeling, and prayer that I had and were acting on them daily. They each had their very own position that they were playing in this game of life I was in, and in this season, I needed all the assistance I could get. My Heavenly Father was heading up the Godhead and was there as an overseer to give instruction and take on all the battles that I passed along to fight for me since I was in no shape, nor did I have the energy, to do it myself.

My Lord and Savior, Jesus Christ, was there to remind me that I was *not alone* in this. He constantly reminded me that, even though it seemed like I was walking this walk by myself, He had walked it before. He was right there with me each step of the way, feeling my hurt and pain, understanding how betrayed I felt, and there to take the edge off my wounded and broken heart. The Holy Spirit was there to be my guide, my comforter, my intercessor, my peacemaker, and to provide me with calm in my darkest moments. He was there to constantly and consistently provide a direct connection to the Savior and my Father in heaven.

When *I finally* realized that I had the Godhead as my team, backing me up, *that* is when my faith and trust in God grew to a whole new level. I've always believed that God can do anything, and I can ask for anything in the name of Jesus Christ and that the Holy Spirit could dwell within me. *But* I never quite grasped the fact that I could attain the type of spiritual relationship in which I felt them with me all the time. That is when the little bit of unbelief I had shifted for me. And when that shift took place, I felt a *change* within me in that very instant. I mean I *felt* it. It was like a switch was flipped.

Since then, I've changed, and I now can say without a shadow of a doubt that *I trust in god* with *all of my heart*. I *know* that He loves me, sees me, hears me, understands me, and watches over me. I *know* that He has willingly taken on my battles, understanding that I've done all I can do with them, and I need Him for me to be victorious. I *know* that He is constantly working on them in the background while I focus on doing the things in my life that I do have control over. I *know* that He is protecting me and guiding me and that there is absolute truth in the well-known scripture, "No weapon formed against me shall prosper."

Within this trial, what I've come to realize is this: the most important thing to our Heavenly Father is our faith in Him. To see our faith in Him grow to the point when it all comes down to it, what we see doesn't matter because we have complete faith and trust in Him. He wants nothing more than to be there to guide us through this earthly journey. To help us remember the calling, the purpose, the passion that He has put within our hearts. To guide us through this life that is full of bumps in the road, hurdles to jump over, disappointment, regret, and pain. To finally get to a place where we fully understand that even when going through negative situations and hard times, we don't have to fear because His love dwells within us. And we, through His grace, have been given the power and authority to speak into our lives in order to create the life we have envisioned for ourselves.

We often forget that He can be with us all the time if we just ask and invite Him into our lives daily. Just as our earthly parents want to be a part of our lives, so does our Heavenly Father. He wants to be there to not only see us through the ups and downs of life but to also partake in the simple and mundane tasks that we think don't matter. He doesn't want us to just think about Him on Sunday, but He wants us to include Him in our everyday lives and in everything that we do.

We need to remember to put Him first and take heed to all that He does for us on a daily basis. If we will do that, we will start to see our lives change drastically. We will start to feel the difference of when we are relying and trusting in Him and when we aren't. I love how Matthew 6:33 shows how simple it truly is.

> "But seek ye first the king-
> dom of God, and his righteous-
> ness; and all these things shall be
> added unto you" (Matthew 6:33,
> KJV).

When you put God first and trust in Him completely, you will find that the weight of the world
starts to lift from your shoulders. You will begin to
realize that you aren't here within this earthly space
to get accolades, notoriety, and validation from anyone. You are here to love others and show that love
by sharing your gifts, talents, and experiences with
them. You are here to help make their lives better in
only the way that *you* can.

This earthly life is hard. There is no question about that. We all go through stuff, just as our
Heavenly Father, Jesus Christ, and the Holy Spirit
can be our constant companions; *you* can be there for
someone else to help them in their journey.

There are *no* coincidences in this life; everything
happens as it's meant to, and purpose can be found in
all things. And yes, even in the bad things that happen to us and around us. As I've mentioned before,
many times God answers prayers through other people, and they usually have no clue that they are an

instrument in His hands. However, the person they have helped knows without a doubt that they were sent by God in a direct answer to a prayer.

I have a few of those types of stories where God sent someone to me just when I needed them. The person didn't have a reason per se as to why they called or came by except for, "Something told me you might need a visit." or "I just felt like I needed to call you" or "You were strongly on my mind." Those are what I call "God Winks" where he answers our prayers simply by prompting others or providing some other sort of sign that only *you* understand.

I know you've heard the phrase that people are placed in our lives for a reason, a season, or a lifetime. And some of those people that are placed in our life are simply the messenger to let us know that God hears and answers our prayers. The thing we must get is that we need to ask Him to be a part of our lives. We determine how He can work in our lives based on how much we include Him in it. Does He have an invite to your entire home, or is He only invited to the porch or foyer?

The relationship we have is on us and how we invite Him into our lives is a direct indication of how He will show up in them. Because again, He will not force us to have a relationship with Him. He is the same yesterday, today, and forever. If there is any distance that is put in between your relationship with God, it is because you have moved away from Him.

As my mom use to tell me when I was growing up, "We will need Him before He will need us." Did anyone else's mom use that on you? If not, let me explain. It's mostly used when a teen gets mad with their parents and does the teenage temper tantrum. The Mom or Dad (but usually the Mom) will belt out, "You can be mad and not talk to me and even give me the silent treatment, but you will need something from me before I will need something from you."

I remember I used to hate that saying, mostly because I knew she was right. And just like those teens' "wake up call" after that phrase is said, it doesn't take long for us adults to realize that you will most certainly need God before He needs you. And, truth be told, He doesn't need us. He wants a relationship with us because we are His children. We are divine beings living an earthly experience.

When I started thinking of life that way, it automatically brought a sense of confidence and divine love into my spirit. I realized that my biggest issue up to this point was that ego mentality that I had of "I've got this, and I can do it on my own!" It's like God wanted me to learn how to give things over to Him in the small ways so I would easily release the reigns when the *big* tests of life came.

However, that didn't happen. *For years,* it didn't happen. God is all-knowing, and He knew I had everything I needed to *get* this concept in order to move into my calling. He just had to allow for something big to be brought into my life for me to be shaken to my core to get it out of me. I had to be in so much emotional pain, totally in that uncomfortable space, that I *had* to bring someone into it in order to help me get out of it. He *knew* that with this type of a blow, I would finally be still enough to *listen*.

And sure enough, that's when the switch flipped on for me. I knew that I was *not* and had never been alone. The distance had always been put there by me insisting on doing it my way. That now sounds so crazy to me as if *God* doesn't know what's best for me?

Friends, I even remember questioning Him in fear because I knew what *I* wanted. I felt that if I let go of it, He would take it from me completely. I didn't even take into consideration that if I let go, put Him first, and allowed Him in my life, that He would always guide me to my greatest good. I never really understood how to use the power of the Godhead in my life.

But now that I do, I wouldn't trade it for the world. I pray that sharing my experience has helped to open your eyes to know that within the darkest of times, we can learn the greatest lessons and utilize effective spiritual tools that will set us on a whole new journey. A journey without stress and strife, worry and fear but a journey—*our* journey—that is outlined and designed by *God* that no one else has been created to fulfill.

You see, we just need to learn to have faith and believe that the most powerful being who created this universe and everything in it has no problem giving us guidance in our lives. We need not worry about the when's, where's, whys, and how's. Because if our Father in heaven has the power to *speak* things into existence, He clearly has the power to do *anything*.

Once we give whatever it is over to God, we need to move out of the way. Let Him work and trust in Him completely. Embrace the fact that He knows what He's doing. He will never mislead you or steer you wrong, and He will never forsake you. He will forever and always have your back.

He is our light through the darkness. And, if we allow Him to be our eyes in those darkest of times, trust in His infinite and eternal sight, and allow Him to fight our battles with His knowledge of all things, we will finally be able to find peace and happiness in our journey through this life.

> "The Lord shall fight for you, and ye shall hold your peace" (Exodus 14:14, KJV).

Now, take a deep breath and let go.

ABOUT THE AUTHOR

Author Michaelle S. Branch is a wife, mother, grandmother, and above all, a daughter of God. She is a Holistic Lifestyle Coach, advocate of Clean Living, born Perfectionist, Empath, and has always felt the need to help others.

When a trial hit her life like a ton of bricks, she turned to God to help save her from the inner darkness she faced. In coming out of the trial a better and stronger person, she had the strong desire to share the lessons, tools, and results of those trials with others. Michaelle wants nothing more than to give God all the glory. She hopes to help others through whatever trials they may face and let them know they aren't alone.

9 781644 682647